More Bullies in More Books

C. J. Bott

THE SCARECROW PRESS, INC.
Lanham, Maryland • Toronto • Plymouth, UK
2009

SCARECROW PRESS, INC.

Published in the United States of America
by Scarecrow Press, Inc.
A wholly owned subsidiary of
The Rowman & Littlefield Publishing Group, Inc.
4501 Forbes Boulevard, Suite 200, Lanham, Maryland 20706
www.scarecrowpress.com

Estover Road
Plymouth PL6 7PY
United Kingdom

British Library Cataloguing in Publication Information Available

Library of Congress Cataloging-in-Publication Data

Bott, C. J. (Christie Jo), 1947–
   More bullies in more books / C. J. Bott.
      p. cm.
   Includes bibliographical references and index.
   ISBN 978-0-8108-6654-6 (pbk. : alk. paper) —
ISBN 978-0-8108-6655-3 (ebook)
   1. Bullying in schools—Prevention. 2. Bullying in schools—
Bibliography. 3. Bullying in schools—Abstracts. I. Title.
LB3013.3.B685 2009
371.5'8—dc22

                                        2009000923

⊗™ The paper used in this publication meets the minimum
requirements of American National Standard for Information
Sciences—Permanence of Paper for Printed Library Materials,
ANSI/NISO Z39.48-1992.
Manufactured in the United States of America.

Contents

Preface

If a student is afraid of being picked on, bullied, or harassed because that student is from a different culture; is female; has a different shade of skin; speaks with a stutter or a foreign or regional accent; is older or younger; practices an unfamiliar religion or has a different gender identity or sexual orientation; is too tall, short, thin, or heavy; wears glasses; has too many pimples; is richer or poorer; doesn't understand as quickly as the other students; has an intense relationship with a computer; wears secondhand clothes, all black clothes, or cheap tennis shoes; or has hair that stands straight up and is midnight blue—that student will not be able to fully operate in the school environment. So without trying any of your skills, you face failure—because like that student, you cannot do your job in an atmosphere of fear.

Our first priority is to keep all of our students safe so that they can learn.

Acknowledgments

First, I want to thank all the authors and publishers who have spotlighted the problem of bullying with an increasing number of bully books. I am grateful for their foresight and commitment to bringing this problem into the spotlight and their willingness to send me their books.

To Ed Kurdyla at Scarecrow, because when I sent him the proposal for this book, he responded with a simple, "It's about time."

There are many others who have helped me in this process, but I must express special thanks to my writers group—Holly Burgess, Carole Kovach, Darla Wagner—for their continued inspiration and helpfulness; to LaQuita Timberlake and Renee Caminati, who helped me sift through tons of books; to my book group, especially Brenna Friesner, for giving me titles; to my friends Mary DiGiovanni and Carol O'Kane, who waited patiently for me to finish so we could go shopping; and to Don Gallo, my first and last reader, my best friend and life partner.

Introduction

So why write a second book?

It's not me, it's the topic, and it isn't going away. Bullying just keeps making headlines, and more people, particularly parents, are growing concerned. State governments are starting to take notice; several have created "anti-bullying legislation," though we all know that won't solve much. In the United States of America, the government spends a great deal of time and money setting up testing that measures the minimum achievement of our students. Thousands of students never achieve those minimum levels. I don't have any statistics that could explain how many of our students fail to reach their potential because the school environment lacks the most basic ingredient in learning—a student's need to feel safe and secure. I will always believe safety is the primary responsibility of every teacher, administrator, and school staff member, as well as of all parents.

Since my first book, *The Bully in the Book and in the Classroom*, was published, I have established a website, www.bulliesinbooks.com. In response to both of these, I have heard from parents, authors, and publishers, as well as educators. The parents tell me sad stories of their children's harassment and say how they have felt helpless and wished they had heard of these books when their sons or daughters were suffering. Teachers tell me these are great resources because no one has enough time to read all the new children's and teen books that contain bullying. They are being published in waves.

Books provide a less threatening way to start a discussion about bullying than an event in the school or a headline in the national news or local newspapers. They also empower teachers and parents, but often the students are the ones who lead us through a book's discussion. And so the need for information about more books is evident.

In *More Bullies in More Books* I have changed the structure. In chapter 1, I talk about the myths we must stop supporting. In chapters 2 through 9, I discuss specific bullying behavior to increase awareness of the range of behaviors that define bullying and to make the books more user friendly for teachers and parents.

Each chapter contains an explanation of the bullying behavior followed by several books (picture books through high school titles) with brief summaries, topics for discussion and/or writing, significant quotes from the text, and finally, an annotated bibliography alphabetized by book title, since most students and teachers remember book titles first. If you can't find a title in a particular level that fits your situation, look in the next section before or after, as many titles overlap. I have tried to focus on books published since 2000 and have included about three hundred annotations. Unfortunately, there are more books than there is time to read them. Over one hundred books are sitting in piles around my office, spilling into the hall, and into the guest bedroom. Those will make it to my website, www.bulliesinbooks.com, eventually. I also want teachers and librarians to have immediate access to the full range of titles that may be needed for a class of students with several reading levels and interest levels. Or a middle school or high school teacher might want to use a picture book for a mini lesson or to introduce a larger unit. Picture books work with everyone. I hope this new format will also educate people to the ever-expanding definition of bullying events—all of which are a threat to an atmosphere of safety and respect.

So I again offer books.

❶

Most People Believe the Myths

Most people believe the myth that bullying in elementary school is only done on playgrounds and is usually just teasing. Other myths support the idea that there are people who deserve to be bullied or that a bully has a poor self-concept. Many still think of a big kid taking a smaller kid's lunch money. Most people do not know that bullying is the generic term for all types of harassment. Most people do not know bullying behaviors start in preschool. Most people do not know that bullying starts with name-calling and can grow as far as physical violence. Most people do not know cyberbullying is the fastest-growing form of bullying in the world. There are still some people who believe bullying is just part of growing up, and what doesn't kill you will make you stronger. Most people do not know the word "bullycide."

Most people are wrong.

Recent research has discredited many of the myths about bullying, and a clearer definition has been established. Bullying happens when

- the behavior is intended to harm or disturb, and this includes embarrassment, or when the targeted person feels harmed, disturbed, or embarrassed.
- the behavior occurs repeatedly and over time.
- there is an imbalance of power.

This definition fits sexual harassment, racial harassment, cultural harassment, or harassment that is based on gender identity, age, ability level, socioeconomic level, academic level, language ability, sexual identity, physical challenges, appearance, or even the type of tennis shoes a person wears. The list goes on. We are an amazing life form, finding many bases on which to build our judgments.

Name-calling starts early, and the first word we use to hurt others is "stupid." Think of a three- or four-year-old you know. Picture that child furiously involved in a conflict with another person of any age as she or he screams, "YOU ARE SO STUPID!" She knows there is power in what she has just done, and she knows that power can hurt. With most three- or four-year-olds, it isn't bullying—but it is practice. As these little ones grow up, they learn other words that can hurt; each is a synonym for stupid. One day as I was giving my tenth graders the homework assignment, one student groaned and said, "Oh, Ms. Bott, that is so gay." I stopped, frowned a bit and asked, "Wait a minute, what part of my assignment is homosexual?" They gasped, "No, Ms. Bott, he just means it's stupid!"

In high school most of the words used in name-calling are much stronger and hurtful—many of them cross the line into hate slurs. And before long the hate-filled words are delivered with physical attacks. It is all bullying.

Often the meanest bully in the school is the one who has grown up with the most privileges but without any empathy. These elite or social-climbing bullies know they look good and have the best wardrobes, the best grades, or the most developed athletic skills. They are also often the teachers' pets. Their elite self-concepts have been nurtured for a long time. There are still some bullies with poor self-concepts, but they are far from the current norm.

Cyberspace has given all of us a new world to explore. We can find answers to any question we have and within a very short time. We can have visual conversations with friends on the other side of the world; we can watch videos of personal moments between people we have never met and probably will never meet. Cyberspace is public and supposedly anonymous, which makes it ripe for bullying. Cyber-humiliation is quick and easy, and teens believe no one can track them down, which allows them to be more cruel than they ever could be if they knew they would be held accountable. Cyberbullying doesn't just happen in one classroom, or in one school building, or on one computer—it reaches around the globe.

As bullying has become more widespread and vicious, some targeted young people have chosen what they believe is their only way out of the daily torture. Bullycide is when a person commits suicide because the bullying is too painful to face, and death is better than the pain, humiliation, and loneliness that come with being bullied. There are no known statistics about bullycide; as with suicide it is difficult to gather information. But as of this writing (October 24, 2008) a Google search for the word "bullycide" offers 16,300 links.

One day I was working with a seventh grade class where all agreed bullying was a problem in their school. Not a huge problem, but definitely a present problem. I asked the students to close their eyes and count up the number of bullies they knew by name or face. Most students' answers fell between 15 and 20. Then I asked them to count up how many students were targeted. Again the answers fell between 15 and 20 in the class of approximately 300. We did the math on the board and decided that left 260–270 students watching these events. The room got very quiet as we all thought about that. Then someone said, "You know, there's more." Unsure what she meant, I responded, "Tell me." "Well, the teachers, hall monitors, custodians, lunch monitors, coaches—they all watch, too." And research supports what that seventh grade class realized that day: the largest part of the school population are silent observers, and far too often silent adult observers.

If you are marketing a bully prevention program, who would you gear it toward for the greatest impact on the environment? A program that involved over 85 percent of the people in the building or a program working with the 10–15 percent of bullies and their targets? Too many schools choose the latter, and they assign it to the counseling department, if they are lucky enough to have one. That. Does. Not. Work. We all know that, have lived it, and still we try it again. That is one definition of insanity.

Only the people who live in the environment can change that environment. A one-day workshop with an education consultant who works specifically with this problem will have a lasting effect of twenty-eight days unless that event fits into an already present and functioning prevention program. Outsiders alone cannot change the school. I no longer accept consulting jobs with schools that do not have a diverse school committee that works on nurturing respectful treatment of each other.

The simple little book *Not My Fault*, written by Leif Kristiansson and illustrated with line drawings by Dick Stenberg (Alhambra, CA: Heryin Books, 2006), is accessible and appropriate for every age group up to and beyond mine. In it a group of fourteen children have witnessed a classmate being physically bullied. To the unspoken question, "What did you do?" each one explains his or her reaction or lack of action. Some blame the targeted kid, some excuse their behavior with a but-everyone-was-doing-it attitude, some were too frightened to act, some just looked away, some say maybe it was the kid's fault, but all agreed—it wasn't their responsibility. The story ends with one question, "Does it have nothing to do with me?"

When do we teach that it does?

2

The Power of Words: Name Calling, Put-Downs, Gossip

Words hold power. We learn that while very young, and the first word we all learn that carries the power to hurt is the word "stupid." Though little kids do not understand the power, they know it hurts. Because when someone calls them "stupid," it hurts them. As we grow up there are other words that carry the same power. Sometimes they are names our family has given us, thinking they are cute. What is cute at two or three rarely stays cute at five or six. "Stupid" is here to stay. If you close your eyes you can picture a little one, furious at mommy or daddy for something, standing with shoulders leaning forward, hands bunched into fists, and screaming, "You are so STUPID!" often followed closely with "and I HATE you!" The power of hurtful words has come into that child's awareness, and it will never leave. The words change, but they all still mean about the same—stupid.

The words we use to attack others carry the same power, anger, or disgust we found in the word "stupid." Although stupid stays as the all-time offender, hurtful words change as the child grows. The names become crueler, the force behind them stronger, and the public humiliation more destructive. The power of twenty-six letters, arranged and rearranged, is amazing.

The book that speaks to this problem the best is James Howe's *The Misfits*, which came out in 2001 and started a movement. In the book (see page 12 for a fuller explanation), four middle school students—Bobby, Joe, Skeezie, and Addie—are called names every day. Bobby and Addie have been friends since birth, and then Joe joined their friendship and finally Skeezie. They are the

Misfits, and one day they totaled up all the names they get called at school. Addie's list has eleven names. Skeezie's list contains sixteen names. Bobby has seventeen names on his list. But Joe has twenty-six names to face at school nearly every day. That is painful, growth-stunting, and humiliating harassment—but they have each other. This election year at school they decide to start an independent political party, the No-Name Party, and their slogan is "Sticks and stones may break our bones, but names will break our spirit." They do not win the election, but their principal, so impressed with their no name-calling campaign, helps them establish a No Name-Calling Day. Howe's publisher, Simon and Schuster, along with GLSEN (Gay, Lesbian and Straight Education Network) and other partnering groups, organized the first No Name-Calling Week in March of 2004. Since then, No Name-Calling Week has been held every January. Today when I checked the website, www.nonamecallingweek.org, there were forty-nine coalition partners.

Many other books also deal with hurtful words. *Hen Hears Gossip* by Megan McDonald shows what happens in a barnyard when Hen hears Pig whispering to Cow. It reminds me of the old telephone game—people sit in a circle and one person whispers a sentence into the next person's ear, who then whispers it into the next person, and so on around the circle. The last person has to say the phrase aloud, and it is never anywhere near the original sentence. An intermediate book, *Amelia's Guide to Gossip* by Marissa Moss, covers many sides of gossip in a brightly illustrated, hand-written journal. Trudy Ludwig deals with the difference between teasing and hurting in her picture book *Just Kidding*. Vince says unkind things all the time and then just says, "Hey, I'm only kidding."

Both *Poison Ivy* by Amy Goldman Koss and *Sticks and Stones* by Beth Goobie deal with name-calling that targets a particular student. In Koss's book, Ivy has been called Poison Ivy since elementary school; it has even spread from the girls' clique that started it to the rest of the students. In *Sticks and Stones*, Jujube gets labeled a slut because Brent leads his buddies to believe he and Jujube have had sex. Jujube fights for her reputation, but Ivy gives up.

Words hold power. Different words hold power over each one of us based on our history, gender, appearance, habits, intellect, and any number of things. Words are how we learn to hurt others and how to control them. What some forget is that every word that comes out of an individual's mouth defines that individual. We are each known by the words we say, and we need to choose those words very carefully.

FOCUS BOOKS

Picture Books

Hen Hears Gossip by Megan McDonald, illustrated by Joung Un Kim. New York: Greenwillow Books, 2008.

> *"Psst. Psst. Psst." Pig whispered something to Cow. Gossip! Hen loved gossip!*

Hen is looking for bugs when she hears Pig whispering to Cow. Hen loves gossip, so she listens to their conversation and then runs to tell her friends. She tells Duck, who runs to tell Goose, who runs to tell Turkey. Turkey tells Hen exactly what she heard. "Hen! You're lazy, fat, and ate all the corn!" Hen gets upset. Then they go back to all their other friends to see how the story got so twisted. They all finally realize that Hen had heard, "A baby calf has been born."

Topics for Discussion

1. Try the old game of Telephone. With students sitting in a circle, whisper a simple sentence to the one on your right, who whispers it to the next person, who does the same until it comes back to you. Usually the sentence gets distorted in the retelling.
2. Why were Cow and Pig whispering?

3. How does Hen react when Turkey said she was "lazy, fat, and ate all the corn!"?
4. Look at the words the animals think they heard and compare them to what was said to them. How do they get the words confused?
5. Why is it that when people whisper, everyone thinks they are gossiping? Are they?
6. There is an old saying: Believe half of what you see and none of what you heard. Why is that a good rule?

Quotes for Reader Response

- *"Psst. Psst. Psst."*
- Hen loved gossip!
- "I didn't say THAT!"

Just Kidding by Trudy Ludwig, illustrated by Adam Gustavson. Berkeley: Tricycle Press, 2006.

> *What's the matter D. J. . . . can't you take a joke? I was just kidding.*

D. J. was the new kid just a month ago when Vince started his put-downs, saying things that made the other boys laugh but that embarrassed D. J. After Vince plays his joke or uses a word put-down, he says he is just kidding. But D. J. doesn't enjoy Vince's "jokes." Eventually D. J. tells his dad about the way Vince teases. Dad suggests they role-play the situation. One person plays the teaser and the others try to respond without saying anything mean back to him.

Vince doesn't stop his verbal attacks on D. J. after Vince tries his dad's strategy, so D. J. and his father meet with his teacher, Mrs. Winter.

More information and questions for discussing the story are provided at the end of the book.

Topics for Discussion

1. What is the difference between teasing and telling?
2. What reward does Vince get from the other kids when he "jokes" with D. J.?
3. What is the difference between teasing and putting people down?
4. When teasing doesn't feel good, it's not teasing. What is it?
5. If you tease a friend, but you see on his face that your words did not feel good, what do you need to do?

Quotes for Reader Response

- "We'll play two out of three," says Vince to Cody. "Loser gets D. J. . . . ready? Rock . . . paper . . . scissors!"
- "Did ya hear that guys?" Vince called out. "D. J.'s gonna be our new *girlie*?"
- "I try to ignore him so he'll stop, but he doesn't," I say. "Then I end up looking like I'm the jerk because I can't take a joke."
- Nick goes first to show me how the game is played and calls Dad "four eyes." "You're right," says Dad. "Wearing glasses is like having an extra set of eyes. Thanks for noticing."
- "Hang out with kids who make you feel good about yourself."

Little Zizi by Thierry Lenain, illustrated by Stéphane Poulin, translated by Daniel Zolinsky. El Paso: Cinco Puntos Press, 2008.

> *Martin was completely naked, frozen in the back of his little stall. Adrian burst out laughing. "Look at the little zizi!"*

One morning Martin and his class are at the swimming pool. Standing in the freezing dressing room, Martin is naked when Adrian opens the door and shouts, "Look at the little zizi!" Loud laughter fills the locker room. Martin slams the door, puts

his clothes on, and waits until everyone has gone. He keeps wondering, why does anyone care how big my zizi is?

When he does open the door, all the boys are still there. Adrian stands right in front of him and tells him that with such a small zizi, he will never be able to make babies. That night Martin has trouble getting to sleep. It's not because he cares that much about babies, but just that day Anais, the girl Martin likes, had asked him how many babies he wanted when he grew up.

There are so many books about girls' concerns about their bodies, a children's book that deals with a boy's concerns about his body is much needed.

Topics for Discussion

1. How does Adrian see Martin's zizi? What does that tell you about Adrian?
2. How do the other boys respond to Adrian's comments about the size of Martin's zizi?
3. Why does Martin want to win the peeing contest?
4. Who wins the contest?
5. What does Anais think of the contest and its winner?
6. How does the little dog in the pictures support Martin?

Quotes for Reader Response

- He wondered if one day his zizi would look like his dad's. But that's normal. All boys wonder about that.
- Martin held back his tears so that he wouldn't be called a girl.

- "The winner will be the one who can pee the furthest." This was Adrian's favorite game.
- She [Anais] passed right by Martin, who didn't dare look at her. Although she did notice his swollen eyes.
- After recess, Martin found the message. It was a heart, a big red heart signed Anais.

Intermediate

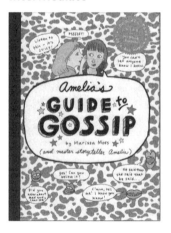

Amelia's Guide to Gossip by Marissa Moss. New York: Simon and Schuster, 2006.

Sometimes the line between news and gossip seems pretty thin to me.

This really looks like a notebook put together by a fifth grader, as it is handwritten with illustrations. Amelia also adds all of her wisdom. She covers Rumor Reading, Urban Legends, Satisfying Gossip, The Gossip Ripple Effect, and What Kind of Gossip Are You? She looks at gossip from a multitude of perspectives.

Topics for Discussion

1. Is there such a thing as truthful gossip?
2. How is spreading gossip like playing that old whispering Telephone game?
3. Why would someone spread a rumor?
4. Why would someone spread a rumor that she knows is a lie?
5. Has anyone ever spread a rumor about you? How did it feel?
6. When does gossip turn mean and hurtful?
7. Does the word "gossip" have a good reputation or a bad one?

Quotes for Reader Response

- And some gossip, even if it's true, you can't repeat or you'll get into trouble.
- Carly says it <u>always</u> hurts the person being talked about because what makes gossip <u>gossip</u> is that it's about things people <u>don't</u> want known.
- Carly says some gossip is like watching clouds—it can change shape right before your eyes.
- That's the bad part of gossip—when people spread stories about you that are horrible lies and the more you deny them, the more people think they're true. But if you ignore the rumors, people will <u>still</u> think they're true.
- An ordinary conversation doesn't go farther than the people speaking to each other—that's the speed of sound. But one juicy whisper can be all over the school by the end of the day—that' the speed of gossip.

Middle School

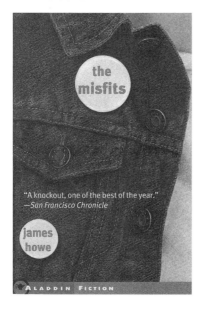

The Misfits by James Howe. New York: Atheneum, 2001.

It doesn't matter how many times I've been called names, it still hurts—and it still always comes as such a surprise that I never know how to respond. Or maybe I do, but I'm afraid. (131)

At Paintbrush Falls Middle School (PFMS), seventh graders Bobby Goodspeed, Skeezie Tookis, Joe Bunch, and Addie Carle have learned to survive with support from each other. Bobby Goodspeed lost his mother a few years earlier, and to cope with that and his father's depression and drinking, Bobby has started eating compulsively. Shortly after his mother's death, he began taking peanut butter and Marshmallow

Fluff sandwiches, his mother's favorite, every day for lunch. He gets called Fluff, Dough Boy, and Roly-Poly. Addie Carle, Bobby's best friend since before they were born because their moms were best friends, is tall, thin, outspoken, and brilliant. She gets called Beanpole, Show-off, Big Mouth, Einstein, and Godzilla. They met Joe Bunch when they were four; he had just moved into Addie's neighborhood. Bobby knocked on Joe's front door, and Joe opened the door wearing a dress, which he flipped up to prove he was a boy. Now Joe paints his pinkie fingernail and gets called Faggot, Fairy, Queer, Tinkerbell, and Pervert. The three of them met Skee-zie Tookis (that's his real name) in kindergarten, but it took them until second grade to get past his bully, tough kid image and form a friendship. Once he had friends, Skeezie stopped making trouble. He did, however, develop a fondness for black leather jackets, slicked-back hair, and haphazard personal hygiene, and picked up labels like Greaser, Wop, Schizo, and Scuz. Others called them losers; they call themselves the Gang of Five (the fifth place is saved for any kid who needs somewhere to belong).

This year is an election year and PFMS has two political parties—the Democrats and the Republicans. These four friends form an independent party with the slogan, "Sticks and stones may break our bones, but names will break our spirit." Their campaign to stop the name-calling not only awakens the students but also the staff. The No-Name Party does not win the election, but they do change the school environment.

This book inspired a movement, No Name-Calling Week, created by Simon and Schuster and GLSEN. The first No Name-Calling Week was in March of 2004. Check out the website, www.nonamecallingweek.org, for more information.

Topics for Discussion

1. All the names Bobby, Joe, Skeezie, and Addie have been called are listed on page 139. Go through the list and identify the ones you have also heard in your school. Add others that you have heard—or used.
2. Make a private list of all the names you have been called. Look at that list and decide if any of those names really do fit you. Write a letter to yourself about how you feel about those names.

3. What single word has power in your life, to change your mood, to make you angry, embarrassed, ashamed? Write a letter to yourself from Bobby or Joe or Skeezie or Addie about how that word can change a life.
4. The Gang of Five spends considerable time cutting down each other. How is that different from when the other kids at school call them names?
5. If you had to run for an office in your school, what would be your slogan?

Quotes for Reader Response

- But all I can say is that if you are willing to dig below the surface, you will discover the real Skeezie Tookis, and there you will find as big a heart as was ever produced by the little town of Paintbrush Falls, New York. (2)
- Names come Addie's way, too, only in her case it is because of her being so tall, in addition to the factor of her intelligence, both of which fall on the plus side of the ledger if you happen to be a boy and are major liabilities if you were born into the world a girl. (11)
- As for Joe, well, he's been called more names than the world's most stinking umpire. (11)
- I wonder if maybe everybody gets names hung on them for only a little part of who they are. (13)
- Kids who are misfits because they're just who they are instead of "fits," who are like everybody else. (14)
- When you get down to it, thinking of somebody as 100% human seriously gets in the way of hating them. (46)
- I'm well on the way to totally betraying my lifelong friendship with Addie for the buzz I'm feeling from having actually made a certifiable popular person laugh with me and not at me. (84)
- DuShawn: That's so gay, y'know, weird.
  Addie: I <u>hate</u> that expression. Gay does <u>not</u> equal weird. (88)
- Skeezie: So does being cool mean you get to go around calling other people names? (91)
- I'm thinking there's a lot more to all of us than the names we're called or what we show on the outside. (121)

- This business of really knowing people, deep down, including your own self, it is not something you can learn in school or from a book. (124)
- "Sticks and Stones may break our bones, but names will break our spirit." (142)

Poison Ivy by Amy Goldman Koss. New Milford, CT: Roaring Brook Press, 2006.

> *They've been calling me "Poison Ivy" for so long that when I refer to myself as just Ivy, it sounds blunt and shortened, even to my own ears. That's how bad it has gotten. (8)*

Ivy Jones tries to make it through the hall before "the Anns" see her and start their harassing. Since fourth grade, when they started calling her "Poison Ivy," Ann, Benita, and Sophie have made her life miserable. Now everyone calls her Poison Ivy like that is her real name. She hates that name, the Anns, and everyone else. She just wants to be invisible.

Ms. Gold, Ivy's teacher for government, somehow hears about her torment and wants Ivy to bring charges against Ann, Benita, and Sophie in a civil court case that Ms. Gold wants to stage in a class role play. Ivy does not want to do it, but Ms. Gold convinces her that if the other girls are found liable, the nightmare will end. Reluctantly Ivy agrees.

As the trial unfolds, it becomes obvious to everyone but Ms. Gold that the jury will find the three not liable because the students are afraid of the consequences Ann will hand out, even though, but also because, they have all seen these three girls make Ivy's life miserable for years. During the trial, Ivy seems to slip farther away each day.

When I first read this book, I was furious with the teacher and the not guilty verdict, but Deborah Brodie, a friend and freelance editor, convinced me that the discussions the book would support gave it power. She was right.

Topics for Discussion

1. When Ms. Gold first talks to Ivy, what emotional state is Ivy in?
2. What are Ms. Gold's objectives for this class project? Does she achieve them?
3. Besides Ann's power as leader of the popular girls, what else works against Ivy?
4. List the main characters and explain the importance of each of their roles.
5. School is enemy territory for Ivy. What is her home life like?
6. Explain the difference between a civil trial and a criminal trial.
7. Apply the Eggshell Head doctrine (115) to this book.
8. The students' points of view are all slanted through their insecurities, fears, pressures, and self-definitions. How could this project be made more effective?
9. Who shares the responsibility for this verdict?
10. How does Ivy deteriorate during the trial?
11. What is the overall effect of this trial project?
12. How would you have voted if you were on the jury?

Quotes for Reader Response

- I told Ms. Gold how The Evil Three have been after me, feeding off me since fourth grade. How they'd practically moved inside my skull, making me hear their insults even when they're nowhere around. (7)
- On some level, we were all so accustomed to Ivy being mistreated that we didn't even recognize it as wrong. (17)
- That's the difference between us. We're both friendless and lonely—but I admit and accept it. And, although I don't like it, I accept that everyone already hates me for whatever mysterious reasons people hate each other. (29)

- Owen pointed to the Anns with their desks pushed together and said, "Do you think they're guilty of bullying, Ivy?" "Well, du-uh," Bryce said. "They only, like pick on her constantly, dude. Everybody knows that." (35)
- An essential part of The Evil Three phenomenon was that it worked only in groups of two or more. Tormenting me was a spectator sport, performance art. Without each other as an audience, I wasn't worth their individual effort. (49)
- But if I won, then Ann and her coven wouldn't be allowed anywhere near me; that heaven would be well worth this bit of ugliness. And if they really were kept from ever speaking to me again, that would be peace everlasting. (92)
- Once or twice, Ms. Gold asked the class to be more respectful, but she didn't demand it. I kept expecting her to come to her senses and put an end to the whole atrocity, but she never did. It didn't seem possible that this was what she'd had in mind from the start, unless she was seriously twisted. (103)
- Our third-hour Government class has made a mockery of the American judicial system from end to end. (138)
- I looked around the lunchroom for a place to eat and saw Einstein, alone, with her nose in a book, as always. In the center of the room, Ann's people held a place for her. They waved frantically, all smiles. And way over there in the corner, at Ivy, staring dimly into space. For one woozy second, the imbalance and shakiness of it all made me want to grab Ann's hair, twist it into a noose, and just strangle her with it. (154)
- And Ms. G amazed me too. Where did she get off looking shocked? Like this wasn't the way everyone always *knew* it would turn out? (166)

High School

Sticks and Stones by Beth Goobie. Victoria, BC: Orca Soundings, 2002.

> *There, on the bathroom wall, someone had written my name. Not just once—several times. A lot of other things were written around it: SLUT, FOR A GOOD TIME CALL JUJUBE GELB,*

Sticks and Stones

Beth Goobie

orca soundings

my phone number. In one corner, different girls had added comments about me, one after the other. It was all the usual stuff, but this time it was about me. (43)

Fifteen-year-old Jujube Gelb has had a crush on Brent for years, and when she finds herself in his arms at the school dance, everything feels magical. When he excuses himself to check on the band, she starts talking with her friend, Carlos, who comments about her being at the dance with "Mr. Warp Speed." Jujube is stunned, but Brent returns then and asks her to go out to his car with him. Nothing happens in his car other than a few kisses, but back inside, everyone is waiting to see their return. Brent walks in with a big grin on his face.

By Monday morning, the word has spread that they had sex. But Jujube doesn't know that when she walks in, and a boy asks if she feels like a new woman. Another guy calls her "Back Seat Baby." In the cafeteria, she hears, "He said you were a ten at the dance, Jujube. No—in the parking lot. A Perfect score. A real pro" (24). Carlos confirms her fears by telling her she is the latest gossip.

When she walks into the girls' bathroom, she finds the walls covered with slurs and put-downs about her. She is too stunned to be hurt and gets Carlos to stand guard for her while she checks out the boys' restrooms, where she finds more of the same. Brent's name is not on any of the walls.

Many students are labeled early in their school lives and the labels stick for a very long time. As with Jujube, the labels are usually wrong, but no one ever bothers to correct the error. Words can destroy a reputation or create one, and often have little to do with truth.

Topics for Discussion

1. On her date with Brent, Jujube is trusting of him. Why does she feel that way?
2. Why does Carlos tell Jujube Brent's nickname?
3. As the rumors spread about Jujube, what kind of rumors spread about Brent?
4. Is there a double standard in the way males and females are expected to behave in the dating world?
5. Carlos is a very kind person. What has been his history in his school?
6. If a girl is called a slut, what is a boy called?
7. When Jujube first sees the words about her on the bathroom walls, what happens inside her?
8. Why is name-calling such an effective way to hurt someone?
9. Why do only the boys know Brent's nickname?
10. In the end, Jujube has gotten stronger and wiser. How has Brent changed?

Quotes for Reader Response

- "He said you were a ten at the dance, Jujube. No—in the parking lot. A perfect score. A real pro." (24)
- Carlos shrugged. "Some guys lie about that stuff all the time. They think if they don't score, they're nobody. So they lie." (26)
- "Look, you can let scum run you or you can let them run each other. Just walk in there now like you're the truth and they're the lies." (28)
- Even if Brent was the one spreading those lies, he was making me wear them. Unreal—the whole thing felt so unreal. (31)
- It feels like it's true, Carlos. Once they say it, that's the way it feels. I *know* it's not, but it *feels* like if everyone's saying it, somehow it must be true. (38)
- As I walked around the walls snapping pictures, something happened. It was as if, somewhere, I was stepping over an invisible line. As if I was finally saying to everyone, "You can't make me take this anymore." As if I had my life back and was I ever going to make it move. (67)

- "Everyone knows a slut isn't really a human being. She's something you kick around and take dirty pictures of. You can laugh, say something you want about her because she's not like you anymore. Maybe she used to be. Maybe she used to be a normal, regular kid. But then someone called her a slut and turned her into a thing. A *nothing*." (78)
- *Slut*. That word could ruin my life . . . *if I believed it*. (79)
- Brent took a few steps back. "Hey, it was just a joke. Why'd you have to take it so personally?"
  "For you, it was a joke. For me, it was my life." (85)

ANNOTATED BIBLIOGRAPHY

Some books are appropriate for other levels; I = intermediate grades, M = middle school, H = high school. Books discussed at length elsewhere in this text are noted parenthetically.

Picture Books

Betty Lou Blue by Nancy Crocker, illustrated by Boris Kulikov. New York: Dial Books, 2006. All the children tease Betty Lou and call her names because she has huge feet, but when a snowstorm blows in, only Betty Lou can carry them to safety.

The Bully from the Black Lagoon by Mike Thaler, illustrated by Jared Lee. New York: Scholastic, 2004. Hubie hears the rumors that the new kid, Butch Pounder, is a terrible bully and his fears starts to build. But when Hubie meets Butch, he realizes Butch is an okay guy.

The Day Leo Said I HATE YOU! by Robie H. Harris, illustrated by Molly Bang. New York: Little, Brown, 2008. Leo's mom keeps saying stop because Leo couldn't stop doing what he shouldn't. Then he yells at Mommy," I HATE YOU!" As soon as he says it, Leo knows how powerful those words are.

Hats by Kevin Luthardt. Morton Grove, IL: Albert Whitman, 2004. The dialogue in this book consists of only thirteen words, which proves how powerful words can be. It only takes one or two words to make a person feel really bad or really good.

Hen Hears Gossip by Megan McDonald, illustrated by Joung Un Kim. New York: Greenwillow Books, 2008. Hen hears Pig and Cow whispering, and she runs to tell what she thinks she heard, but she had the words confused. Soon everyone is upset and Hen has to find out what Cow really said. (See page 7.)

Here Comes Smelly Nellie by Terry Slater, illustrated by Marilee Harrald-Pilz. New York: Scholastic, 2007. Nellie Higgenbottom accepts that her brother calls her funny names, but when the kids at school start calling her names, it doesn't feel much like fun. The book ends with the question, "What would you do if a bully or a group of kids called you names?" A teacher guide is on the back cover.

I Get So Hungry by Bebe Moore Campbell, illustrated by Amy Bates. New York: Penguin, 2008. Arnold calls Nikki names like Supersize to get a laugh from the other students. Nikki doesn't like being overweight, but until she sees her teacher walking everyday before and after school, she doesn't have any hope that she can change and stop the name calling.

Just Kidding by Trudy Ludwig, illustrated by Adam Gustavson. Berkeley: Tricycle Press, 2006. Vince likes to make D. J. the target for his jokes and then he yells, "Just kidding." Like most kids, D. J. feels put down, but then he learns some good counter moves from his dad and older brother. A bit didactic, this book will work with younger students and educate the adults who need to know how to help. (See page 8.)

Little Zizi by Thierry Lenain, illustrated by Stéphane Poulin, translated by Daniel Zolinsky. El Paso: Cinco Puntos Press, 2008. While the boys are changing after swim class, Adrian sees Martin naked and announces to everyone that Martin has a little zizi. Besides repeating that, he also tells Martin he will never be able to make babies. (See page 9.)

Never Tease a Weasel by Jean Conder Soule, illustrated by George Booth. New York: Random House, 2007 (originally published 1964). A rhyming story that tells of fun things to do for others, but warns to never tease.

Purplicious by Elizabeth Kann, illustrated by Victoria Kann. New York: HarperCollins, 2007. Pinkalicious loves the color pink, but the girls at school tell her pink is for babies. Just when she thinks she will never have a friend again, she meets a girl who adds pink to blue to make "Purplicious."

Wings by Christopher Myers. New York: Scholastic Press, 2000. Everyone thinks Ikarus Jackson's wings are ugly, except for one quiet girl who finds her voice to tell Ikarus his wings are beautiful.

Intermediate

Amelia's Guide to Gossip by Marissa Moss. New York: Simon and Schuster, 2006. Amelia talks about all the many dangers of gossip in this hand-written and illustrated guide. (See page 11.)

Backyard Sports: #1 Wild Pitch by Michael Teitelbaum, illustrated by Ron Zalme. New York: Grosset and Dunlap, 2008. Joey MacAdoo loves baseball and he loves winning even more, but he thinks he has to be in charge of everyone. His baseball bossiness is close to destroying his team as his comments turn into put-downs. When does bossiness turn into bullying?

How to Face Up to the Class Bully: Willimena Rules! Rule Book #6 by Valerie Wilson Wesley, illustrated by Maryn Ross. New York: Jump at the Sun, 2007. Willie tries really hard not to get trapped by Irene, the class bully, but she just does not know what to do, until she talks with her parents.

Nothing Wrong with a Three-Legged Dog by Graham McNamee. New York: Random House, 2000. As the only white kid in his fourth grade class, Keath gets called Whitey, Vanilla, and Mayonnaise, and his best friend, Lynda, gets called Zebra because her mom is black and her dad is white.

Racing the Past by Sis Deans. New York: Henry Holt, 2001. Eleven-year-old Ricky gets into fights when bullies taunt him after his abusive father dies in a drunk driving accident. He makes a deal with the principal: to avoid the bullies he will never share the same space with them, which means no recess or school bus. He walks, and then runs, to and from school.

Shredderman by Wendelin Van Draanen, illustrated by Brian Biggs. New York: Alfred A. Knopf, 2004. Noland Byrd has seen Bubba Bixby bully lots of other kids, and he always calls them names. In fact Bubba has names for all the kids; Bubba calls Noland, Nerd, and now everyone calls him Nerd. Then Noland creates a superhero website, Shredderman, and his mission is to expose all of Bubba's evil doings. (See chapter 8, page 152.)

Super Emma by Sally Warner, illustrated by Jamie Harper. New York: Puffin Books, 2006. Emma is the second smallest third grader; only her friend Ellray is smaller. After a substitute teacher calls Ellray by his legal name, Lancelot, bully Jared Matthews cannot resist picking on him, or calling Emma, Super Emma, when she stands up for Ellray. Good adult role models in Emma's mother and the teacher. (I)

Ten Ways to Make My Sister Disappear by Norma Fox Mazer. New York: Arthur A. Levine, 2007. Ten-year-old Sprig thinks her older sister Dakota has never been nice to her since she turned twelve, but they both come to understand how much they need each other. Sibling bullying is exceedingly common, and though the bullying in this book is mild, it will lead to great discussions and maybe some confidence sharing.

Middle School

Crossover by Jeff Rud. Victoria, BC: Orca Sports, 2008. Kyle Evans loves basketball but he also loves theater, and this year the fall production is *Oliver*. After he gets a part he has to deal with an angry coach and a homophobic teammate who sets out to destroy him and Lukas, a perceived-to-be-gay cast member.

Deliver Us from Normal by Kate Klise. New York: Scholastic, 2005. Eleven years old, friendless, and poor, Charles Harrisong feels emotions more deeply than most, particularly the pain of being bullied. He yearns for deliverance and for normalcy, but it is only after his sister's humiliation during her campaign for seventh grade class president that his hopes appear to be realized.

Diary of a Wimpy Kid: A Novel in Cartoons by Jeff Kinney. New York: Amulet Books, 2007. Greg Heffley keeps a journal during his last year in middle school. Not only does he get bullied, but he becomes a bully, too.

The Misfits by James Howe. New York: Atheneum, 2001. Four social outcasts in seventh grade create a third political party and run for student council on a "No Name-Calling" platform. (See page 12.)

Poison Ivy by Amy Goldman Koss. New Milford, CT: Roaring
  Brook Press, 2006. Since fourth grade, when they started calling her "Poison Ivy," Ann, Benita, and Sophie have made Ivy
  Jones's life miserable. Ms. Gold, their government teacher,
  only makes things worse by staging a mock trial on Ivy's
  behalf. (See page 15.)
Teasing: Deal with It before the Joke's on You by Steve Pitt, illustrated by Remis Geoffroi. Toronto: James Lorimer, 2006.
  An excellent resource to use with the younger children who
  keep saying, "But I was just teasing." Nonfiction, part of the
  excellent Deal with It series.

High School

The Brimstone Journals by Ron Koertge. Cambridge: Candlewick
  Press, 2001. Using first-person poems from the points of
  view of fifteen students, Koertge reveals the anger, hate, and
  longings in a suburban high school that lead to an explosive
  situation.
Exposure by Patricia Murdoch. Victoria, BC: Orca Book Publishers, 2006. Julie, a bit overweight and very timid, gets bullied
  by queen bee Dana and her follower, Brynn. Dana says she
  was attacked at the beach party, but Julie knows the truth
  and now has to decide how to use the evidence.
Names Will Never Hurt Me by Jaime Adoff. New York: Dutton
  Children's Books, 2004. A view of what happens in one high
  school on the one-year anniversary of a school shooting,
  told in prose and verse mostly from the perspectives of four
  teenagers, all of whom have been victims of harassment in
  various forms. (M)
. . . Or Not? by Brian Mandabach. Woodbury, MN: Flux, 2007.
  Cassie Sullivan—bright, sensitive, and wise beyond her fourteen years—stands up for her anti-war beliefs in a conservative Christian community filled with right-wing Americans.
  Her school days are tortuous with the other students harassing her verbally and stuffing vicious notes into her locker, but
  she finds solace in her journal writing and the beauty around
  the family's cabin in the mountains. (M)
Sandpiper by Ellen Wittlinger. New York: Simon and Schuster,
  2005. In eighth grade, Sandpiper learned that the easiest way

to get a boyfriend was to offer oral sex. Now in the tenth grade, she is tired of all the gossip and her old reputation, but finds it impossible to change it.

Sticks and Stones by Beth Goobie. Victoria, BC: Orca Soundings, 2002. Falsely labeled as a "slut," Jujube fights back against the slurs whispered in the hallways and written on the bathroom walls of her school. (M) (See page 18.)

Story of a Girl by Sara Zarr. New York: Little, Brown, 2007. Three years earlier, when Deanna was thirteen, her father caught her in a car having sex with a seventeen-year-old, and she has had to live with the whole town labeling her.

The Throwaway Piece by Jo Ann Yolanda Hernandez. Houston: Arte Publico Press, 2006. After years of taking care of her alcoholic mother, Jewel, a gifted loner, finds herself a "state kid" when her mother abandons her for a string of loser boyfriends. Jewel finds herself on a self-destructive path for survival.

Twisted by Laurie Halse Anderson. New York: Viking, 2007. Tyler Miller used to be the invisible boy at school until he spray-painted the high school with obscenities and became the high school weirdo. Not much of an improvement, except now most people leave him alone, except Chip Milbury, elitist bully and brother to Tyler's heart's desire, Bethany.

Whale Talk by Chris Crutcher. New York: Greenwillow Books, 2001. T. J. Jones, an adopted child with a multicultural heritage, pulls together a high school swim team composed of misfits, giving them a place to belong in a school and community filled with discrimination.

❸

Being New, Being Different

It is tough to be new. It is tough to be different. To be both new and different is inhumanly tough. We have all been new at some point in our history. Everyone is new on the first day of kindergarten or first grade. But newness can fade and we become the home team, the older kids, one of the crowd. Being different doesn't fade away, and how different from the norm a person is can be a major influence on how that person will be accepted—if at all.

Another factor is the environment. Some environments are more accepting of differences than others, and some differences seem to be easier to accept. Confusing? You bet. Sit in any school, any grade, any town and watch the new kid or the kid who is "different" enter the lunchroom, that student-dense arena nearly impenetrable to adults (who are another type of different). Watch the face of that student. See the pain, the humiliation, the rejection, or the loneliness. Many of us will experience a flashback to a similar moment in our lives. Teachers can impact that environment by creating an atmosphere of acceptance for each person's uniqueness.

Differences come in many varieties. Some of our most bullied students learn English as their second language. They may still have an accent or be unsure of words or slip into their first language when frustrated, angry, or frightened. In *Losers* by Matthue Roth, Jupiter Jason Glazer, a Russian boy who has been in the United States for several years, still does not feel that he fits in. At a party, a girl tells him how she changed her dialect.

That advice starts Jupiter on one very exhausting weekend of listening to 1950s country music and lounge singers like James Brown, Frank Sinatra, and Sammy Davis Jr., and others right up to the present. He nearly eliminates his accent, and suddenly he has more confidence. Language and verbal skills are vital to acceptance.

Young people use many things to separate the masses. In schools, appearance and clothes are two other measures that kids use to judge. At a time when most teens are fighting to be their own person at home, they want to fit in with everyone at school, and they often do that by dressing like all the others. There really are dress codes for middle school and high school; adults sometimes do not recognize them. Every time I have asked a group of students to diagram the hierarchy of student groups in their school, the top group is always the same—the best-dressed and the best-looking kids. That is one group, not two. It is not enough to be good looking or to have all the right clothes.

Body size—tall, short, thin, thick—puts target signs on many teens. Anyone who doesn't fit the popular image created by TV shows, fashion magazines, or the latest Hollywood kids-gone-wild gets judged, talked about, and excluded. For some teens the physical differences are more serious. I once asked a student who was wheelchair bound how kids treated her in the hall. Did they open doors for her or let her go first? She said it wasn't like that at all. They would walk in front of her and close doors in her face, and some teachers didn't assign her a seat with easy access. Most of the time, people pretended she was invisible.

Money is another great divider, as it can buy the latest clothes, electronic toys, homes, worldly experiences, and even the perfect body makeovers through surgeries. Our society rewards those who have money. Those without are judged by that lack. In *No Castles Here* by A. C. E. Bauer, Augie Boretski is one of two white kids in his class. He lives in a poor neighborhood, with a single mom who works as a waitress—and he wears thick glasses. Augie is an easy target, so the bullies take what little extra he has.

Whitney, in *Home and Other Big Fat Lies* by Jill Wolfson, is on her way to her twelfth foster home in a small northern California logging town. Whitney is so short her foster brother calls her Termite, but she carries inside her a huge spirit that helps her stay centered and rules for survival to help her deal with the label *foster kid*.

David, in *Defect* by Will Weaver, has facial deformities that are enough to make him different, but he also has a secret. Hidden extra flaps of skin between his arms and sides enable him to glide on the wind (see chapter 4, "Body Image").

Out of all the books mentioned in this chapter, the most extreme example of being different is *Generation Dead* by Daniel Waters where some teens have died and come back to life. In this parallel to our society, the dead kids are shunned by most of the school and abandoned by the government, and some by their families. Bioism, the hatred of dead people, becomes the new "ism."

There are more than enough labels in our schools. Besides all the ones mentioned, there are those for race, religion, or sexual identities that are the easiest to assign and can lead into extreme bullying or even hate crimes. (See chapter 6, "The 'Isms,'" and chapter 7, "Homophobia.") Students who are gay and students who are perceived to be gay are the most targeted students in the school. Middle school nurtures the growth of homophobia through ignorance and silence. No teacher, principal, counselor, secretary, or custodian should ever pretend they do not hear the phrases "That is so gay!" or "Faggot."

Whether it is homophobic or racist name-calling, exclusion, or I-am-more-powerful-than-you shoves in the hallway, when an adult witnesses that bullying behavior and does nothing, everyone—the bully, the target, and every student watching—believes that adult supports the bully. Our silence supports the harassment. Bullying, harassment, prejudice all go against the basic standard of respect. As adults we know the rules; we just have to practice them, every day and all the time. That is tough, too.

FOCUS BOOKS

Picture Books

First Day in Grapes by L. King Pérez, illustrated by Robert Casilla. New York: Harcourt, 2000.

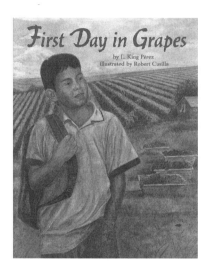

First Day in Grapes
by L. King Pérez
illustrated by Robert Casilla

The pledge made him feel proud to be an American, even though some people treated him like a foreigner.

Chico's family moves around California with the ripening crops, and his first day of third grade is also the workers' first day in grapes. At school he tries to speak only English, but he sometimes slips into Spanish. The day is going well: his teacher Ms. Andrews likes him, he gets through his short introductory speech, and his math skills impress Ms. Andrews, but at lunch Mike and Tony try to humiliate the new kid. Again, his math skills save him.

Topics for Discussion

1. What must it be like to be the new kid over and over again?
2. The first day at school, the teacher has Chico sit next to John Evans. How is John different from most of the other students Chico has met on his first days?
3. Why do Mike and Tony pick on Chico?
4. Define "immigrant."
5. What is your definition of an American?
6. How can a person who is not born in the United States of America become a citizen?
7. Why do you think Chico's mother always puts up curtains each time they move to a new place?

Quotes for Reader Response

- He'd had so many first days—first days in artichokes, first days in onions, first days in garlic. Now his first day in third grade would be in grapes.

- Mamá . . . put one hand on Chico's shoulder, the other on his back. She straightened him up until he looked like Papá before he went to work in the fields each day.
- "Hey, new kid," one of the boys called to Chico. "What are you looking at?"
- Quickly Chico added up the weeks they'd be in grapes. If they stayed through raisins, maybe he'd get to go to the Math Fair.
- Chico didn't feel macho, and he didn't feel brave either.
- Chico jumped off the bus. This had been a pretty good first day.

Trouble for Trudy by Teddy Slater, illustrated by Sally Springer. New York: Scholastic, 2007.

> *Suddenly, a voice shouted, "Hey, Four-eyes!"*

Trudy is the new girl and the other students think she looks weird with her orange hair, thick glasses, and odd clothing—except Annie who likes different. Trudy and Annie become friends, but one day on their way home some kids call Trudy "Four Eyes" and take her glasses. Annie does not know what to do.

Topics for Discussion

1. Have you ever been the new kid?
2. Try to remember how you felt on your very first day in your school. How did you feel?
3. How do you feel in your school now? What has changed?
4. Make a list of all the things Annie could do to help her friend, Trudy.

Quotes for Reader Response

- Trudy had wild orange hair and thick round glasses. Her clothes never matched.

- No one in Trudy's class even tried to get to know her. No one but Annie.
- Trudy and Annie became best friends.
- Suddenly, a voice shouted, "Hey, Four-eyes!"
- Trudy reached for Annie's hand. "Annie?" she called. Annie looked at Trudy.
- She was afraid that if she stood up for Trudy, the bullies would do something bad to her!

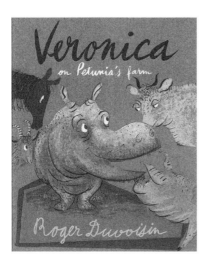

Veronica on Petunia's Farm by Roger Duvoisin. New York: Alfred A, Knopf, 2008 (previously published 1962, 1990).

> *At once she saw it was a lovely place, just right for a hippopotamus.*

Veronica, a very happy hippo, moves to Mr. Pumpkin's farm where none of the other animals will talk to her. She is the first hippopotamus they have ever seen, and they decide that hippopotamuses do not belong on a farm. Petunia the goose notices that Veronica does not look well. All the animals come to their good senses and try to help her.

Topics for Discussion

1. What is the best way for you to welcome a new student to class?
2. Have you ever been the new student? What does it feel like?
3. Why don't the other animals like Veronica?
4. What is gossip?
5. Why is gossiping an unfriendly thing to do?

Quotes for Reader Response

- "Well," said Ida the hen. "I don't like the look of a hippopotamus. It's neither a hen, nor a duck, nor a cow. . . . It has no place on a farm."
- "How ugly it is!" said Pig.
- "Not a farm name," said Goat. "A zoo name. That's what it is."
- "Therefore a foreigner." Said Donkey.
- "I think IT does not look well."
- "Oh . . . I took some thistle to Veronica and I said, 'Good morning,' and do you know what happened? She opened one eye and said 'Good morning' too."
- "Good morning, my friends," said Veronica. And her smile was the biggest hippopotamus smile. Very big.

Yoon and the Jade Bracelet by Helen Recorvits, illustrated by Gabi Swiatkowska. New York: Farrar, Straus and Giroux, 2008.

I wanted so much to jump and sing with them, but I was still the new girl, I had not been invited yet.

Yoon moved to America from Korea, and that makes her feel especially different at school. One day at lunch, an older girl asks if she could sit with Yoon. They talk and she invites Yoon to play jump rope with her, but she also wants Yoon's jade bracelet. Yoon loans it to her thinking they will be friends, but the other girl decides to keep the bracelet and avoid Yoon. Eventually her teacher helps her get the bracelet back.

Topics for Discussion

1. It is always hard to be the new student. List the ways Yoon is new and different in her school.

2. If you were new to the school like Yoon, what would you want most?
3. When the older student sat with Yoon, what did you think would happen?
4. Why did Yoon let the older student wear her special jade bracelet?
5. How does Yoon help the teacher question the girl?
6. When there is a new student in your class, how can you make him or her feel welcome?
7. Why is it important to make new students feel welcomed?

Quotes for Reader Response

- I watched the girls in my school yard turning such a rope and jumping and singing happy songs.
- "You are alone today. I will be your friend. Would you like to play jump rope with me?" the older girl asked.
- "In America friends share things. If we are going to be friends, you should share your bracelet with me."
- I was just like the silly girl in my storybook. I had been tricked by a tiger.
- "The bracelet is a symbol of kindness and courage. It is a symbol of jade friendship—true friendship."
- My teacher's eyes said Older-girl-you-are-in-trouble.
- "Here is your name bracelet, Shining Wisdom."

Intermediate

Drita, My Homegirl by Jenny Lombard. New York: Puffin Books, 2006.

> When you call someone your homey, it's because they feel like a home to you, and you really like them. (23)

Drita and her mother, brother, and grandmother escape from Kosovo and in New York City join her father who had escaped a year earlier. Maxie lives with her father and grandmother. Her mother died in a car accident two years earlier, and Maxie refuses to accept she won't come back. Drita and Maxie are two girls struggling with their lives when they meet in Miss Salvato's class.

With the richness of their cultures and the intensity of fourth grade thinkers, they tell the story in alternating chapters.

At school Drita is quiet, confused, and lonely; Maxie is entertaining, opinionated, and challenging. On Drita's first day, Maxie makes a joke by calling her Drita Drano. Miss Salvato talks privately with Maxie and suggests she research Kosovo for her social studies theme, which Maxie rejects until she sees Brandee pick on Drita. Soon a friendship blooms that involves not only the two girls, but their families become friends, too.

Topics for Discussion

1. List all of the pressures in Drita's life.
2. List all of the pressures in Maxie's life.
3. What are some of the pressures in your life that sometimes make it difficult to concentrate in school?
4. In the beginning, why does Maxie make fun of Drita?
5. What made life difficult for Drita and her family in Kosova?
6. What made life difficult for Drita and her family in the United States?
7. Kosova or Kosovo, who should decide?
8. What is the first thing that makes Maxie want to be friends with Drita?
9. Brandee and Maxie have been friends since second grade. Why does that change?
10. On page 17, Drita talks about her school in Albania and her new school in New York City. How do they compare?

Quotes for Reader Response

- My grandmother is a very wise woman, I think. She knows that when you are sad and far away from home, the best thing to do is to sing in your strongest voice. (6)
- In Albania, there is a wall. On one side are the Serbian children and their teacher, also a Serb. On the other side, that is where we Muslim children sit, with Mr. Shubani our teacher. (17)
- I look over at the new girl who's sitting at my desk. I got to say, I don't like her. I don't like her hair, I don't like her clothes. I don't like her face and I don't like her eyes. She's the kind of white person who's so pale, she's like a ghost—you think you can see right through her. (19)
- Inside I know it is finally happening. The good life my family will have in America is finally beginning. (47)
- How stupid of me to think that these girls would ever like me. No one does, and no one ever will. (59)
- I will not make my shame worse by letting them see me cry. (69)
- For the rest of the day and until bedtime, I think this is my hardest job, to hide the truth from my family. (73)
- "Yes. It is very, very, very hard to walk away from a fight when you know you're right. But that is what you have to do."
  "Why?"
  "Because that's the only way to stop the fighting." (96)
- But then when I got to know Drita, I started finding out that even though on the outside we were different, on the inside we were just the same. (134–35)

Home, and Other Big, Fat Lies by Jill Wolfson. New York: Henry Holt, 2006.

No one had been praying day and night for a kid like me to come live with them. No one wanted me or any of us to stay forever. Home! What a big, fat lie. (84)

Whitney holds her pet pill bug, Ike Eisenhower the Sixth, while sitting in her social worker's car. They are on their way to Forest Glen in northern California, population 1,639. With her strong

temper, inability to keep her mouth closed, ability to stretch the truth, and quick fingers in stores, Whitney is not an easy child to place. She is short for an eleven-year-old, due to a congenital heart problem. The Mc-Crary family, Mr., Mrs., and son Striker, will be her twelfth foster family.

Forest Glen has always been a logging town, but recently the government has shut it down after a rare bird was seen nesting in the area. The men are depressed and the women are trying to keep everything normal. The only way the families are able to pay their bills is to take in foster kids. Whitney has never seen so many foster kids; they make up 20 percent of her class.

Whitney has a wealth of personality and quickly becomes the center of all the foster kids. She also wins over Striker, and he teaches her about the forest and Big Momma, the mother of all the redwoods.

Topics for Discussion

1. What do you think of Termite's social strategy: "Aim for immediate noticeability"?
2. When Termite first arrives at his house, why is Striker so angry with Termite?
3. Why is Termite so excited to meet so many other foster kids in the same school?
4. Why does Josh stay in his box?
5. How does Termite's Top Ten Popularity List change through the book?
6. Termite has never done very well in school because she never stayed in one place for very long. How does the reader know she really is very smart?

7. Striker and Termite were almost enemies; how do they become friends?
8. Why does it seem particularly unfair to pick on foster kids? Or is it?
9. In her The Story of a Tree Cone #1 assignment (starting on page 141), Termite writes with a tiny "w," and it is the only letter in lower case. Why does she do that?
10. Termite has really found a family and a place to belong. Why does she jeopardize that by trying to save Big Momma?

Quotes for Reader Response

- Nobody understands that when you move around a lot like I do, there's something really nice about having my clothes smell like me. (19)
- I let those words return to give me good advice. *People can say hurtful things, Whitney, but that doesn't mean you have to get hurtful back.* (35)
- I must have started ten new schools in my life, and I don't think you ever really get over wanting to run off somewhere and puke about it. (49)
- Once you know something special about a kid, or a rock, you can never look at them the same. (56)
- Some people act like *foster* is a dirty word . . . —like it's my fault that I had the dumb luck to be born to parents that I never met. Even some foster kids are like that. (59)
- "Maybe foster kids are like lepers to some people." (70)
- Still, no matter how they dress, popular kids definitely give off a certain aroma, which is my way of saying that they act like their farts don't smell. (71)
- Mr. Cator didn't seem to think there was anything unusual about treating the most annoying kid in the class like she was a genius nature girl. (118)
- Striker and me, two kids from different worlds, standing up—no sitting down—for something much bigger than either one of us. (264)
- Can an outsider become an insider? (281)

Middle School

Egghead by Caroline Pignat. Calgary: Red Deer Press, 2008.

> *No Difference*
> *I am*
> *not all that different*
> *from you.*
>
> *Unless you consider that*
> *I am*
> *the only one*
> *who isn't*
> *trying to be the*
> *same. (76)*

Three ninth graders, Will Reed, Katie McGillvary, and Devan Mitchell, tell this story in alternating chapters. Devan and Katie tell theirs through narration, while Will's is told through poems.

Will is the odd student; his mother recently died and he has lost himself in an interest in bugs by creating and nurturing an ant farm for his science project. The ants treat him nicer than most of the students. Shane, an equal opportunity bully, picks on everyone, but he focuses on Will the most.

Katie, Will's science partner and good friend, witnesses how Shane and his thugs bully Will, and sometimes she tries to stop it. She also encourages Will to stand up to Shane, but he is too frightened and wisely chooses not to, as Shane would only escalate his bullying.

Devan, one of Shane's thugs, does not think for himself. He just does what Shane says, and seems to think the bullying is fun—until he learns more about Will and starts to doubt his role in the harassment.

Topics for Discussion

1. What is home life like for Will, Katie, Devan, and Shane?
2. Of the four of them, which one has the most difficult home life?

3. What behaviors does Shane use to bully the other kids and Will?
4. Shane leads it, but how are Brad and Devan responsible for the bullying?
5. Why won't Will tell the principal what Shane does to him?
6. Which character changes the most in the book?
7. When Shane finds Katie alone in the science room, he grabs her arm and then Devan walks in. What does Devan say to Shane to make him stop, and why did those words work?
8. What gives Devan the confidence to confront Shane?
9. In Will's last poem (171), what is his message to Katie?

Quotes for Reader Response

- Shane got right up in Martin's face. "Still a total loser, eh, Ma-ma-ma-martina? Somethings never change." (13)
- Then Shane followed the guy around the store, snorting and grunting like a pig. Man. I nearly wet my pants laughing. But that's Shane for you. He cracks everyone up. Well, maybe not the fat kid. (14)
- My heart pounded in my throat. I took a step back. Just a little one. Hardly noticeable to anyone else. But somehow, that couple of inches told Shane all he needed to know. His mouth slithered into a cold smile. (18)
- And there is / no teacher's manual / on me. (35)
- "Where are you getting all the panties?" . . .
  "How do I know?" he goes. "I just brought the first pair."
  Leave it to Shane to start a new tradition. (37)
- I thought she was concerned about me, but as I walked on to Will's house, I realized what she was really saying. Jenna wouldn't be my friend if I was Will's. (53)
- "Shut your mouth, fag!" Shane yells, as he and Brad barge in. He grabs the roll of duct tape off the table and sticks a strip across Egghead's mouth. (72)
- If only she knew. I'm *not* a winner. I'm the loser who stood by and did nothing. (93)
- I was never a great friend to Will. I admit it. But nothing, nothing was worse than what I had done. I stepped out of

the spotlight and pushed through the crowd—horrified at the realization. I was one of them now. (109)

- Shane did the pushing, but I'm guilty, we all are, for letting him. I stood by all those times, just watching Will get pushed over the edge. I didn't *do* anything. And that is why I owe Will. (132)

- Suddenly I understood. I saw how it must have been for Will all those months. *Stand up to him. Don't let him push you around. Don't give him power over you.* Those "strategies" echoed hollow and empty in my head. It was a lot easier to give that advice than to take it. (156)

- "You can't change other people, Devan. Not Shane or Brad or anyone else for that matter." Dad says. "The only person you can change is yourself. And that takes work." (164)

No Castles Here by A. C. E. Bauer. New York: Random House, 2007.

> "*You can't always run away from your problems, Augustus. They have a way of following you.*" *(104)*

Augie Boretski spends most of his time hiding out at home, while his mom works at the Pear Hill Diner. One of two white kids in his sixth grade class, Augie knows more bullies than friends. Dwaine Malloy, Fox Tooth Green, and Sergio Barnaby are the worst. They take his lunch money or his lunch and sometimes they wait for him after school. They all live in the same neighborhood in Camden, New Jersey.

On one of the last summer days before school starts, Augie counts up all his change to buy a train ticket into Philadelphia, where he discovers a magical bookstore. There he finds a dark green book with gold lettering on the cover, and when he touches the illustrations and lettering inside, they seem to come to life.

His real life involves a really cool Big Brother that he can't keep because he's gay and the bullies will mess with both of them; the newly formed Junior Choir, which helps Augie gain confidence and friends; a paralyzing ice storm that destroys part of the school; and a new sense of community that grows out of the destruction.

No Castles Here is really two stories: one story is Augie's life and the other story hides inside that book. They weave around each other, trading lessons until they overlap. And for that book's wonderful fantasy that mesmerizes Augie, you will have to read the book.

Topics for Discussion

1. Augie may be a target in his neighborhood, but he isn't afraid of everything. List examples of his courage and willingness to try new things.
2. What keeps Augie from becoming part of the neighborhood bullies?
3. Mr. Franklin treats everyone in his chorus as equals. How does that affect the students? How does that affect the relationship between Augie and Sergio?
4. Why do Dwaine and Fox Tooth start bullying Sergio?
5. Why does the author use both Augie's story and Louisa's story to tell her story?
6. Both Augie and Louisa go through bad times, and their defense was to hide from the world. How did each become visible?
7. Augie learns that his Big Brother, Walter, is gay. What is Augie afraid might happen if the street gang finds out?
8. What is Augie's school community like in the beginning of the book? What is that community like at the end of the book? How did people change that community?
9. When you belong to a group of people, you are judged by the behaviors of that group. Sergio changes groups. How does his reputation change?
10. How does joining together to repair the school benefit everyone?

Quotes for Reader Response

- Too bad his life was filled with miserable beginnings. (49)
- Augie never saw the punch, but he felt Dwaine's fist as it landed in his stomach. As he fell to the ground, Fox Tooth shielded them from the playground monitor's view. (62)
- "Drop him," Sergio ordered. Even before Augie hit the ground, Fox Tooth had started kicking. Augie curled up tight into a ball, but Fox Tooth only kicked harder around his shoulders and head. One of the kicks grazed an ear and knocked his glasses clear down the alley. He swallowed a scream; it felt as if his ear had been ripped off.
  "Next time, you have something," Sergio hissed, "or we'll check out your insides." (68)
- What I need, Augie thought, is a fairy godmother. (80)
- Louisette's eternal youth made people whisper. She became a target for those who see evil, even when there is none. (139)
- "Something good has begun to roll," Mr. Franklin continued. "It isn't time to put on the brakes." (149)
- "Do you think people always hide who they are?" (158)
- Dwaine was the reason Augie had told Walter to leave. Walter had done nothing wrong—in fact, he had tried to help. . . . Keeping him out of his life because of narrow-minded bullying Dwaine was stupid. (160)
- "Why stop something good because something bad's gotten in the way?" (226)
- There might be no castles in his neighborhood, but this was his home. He'd do what he could to keep it whole. (244)

High School

Generation Dead by Daniel Waters. New York: Hyperion Books, 2008.

They are the people that some of you, and many outside the walls of this school, would refer to as zombies, corpiscles, dead heads, the undead, worm food, shamblers, *the* living dead, *the* Children of Romero, *and a whole host of other pejorative names designed to hurt and marginalize. (101)*

A strange phenomenon has begun. Some teens have died and then have returned to life. No explanation has been found, and the number of undead, living impaired, or differently biotic kids keeps growing. Many of them are not welcomed back! Some parents even abandon their sons or daughters. The government does not know what to do with them, and the undead do not have any rights because they are considered—dead.

Adam Layman, more than just a football jock, and Phoebe Kindall, more than just a goth girl, lead in accepting the undead as they enroll in Oakvale High School. Peter Martinsburg does the opposite by leading the harassment. Tommy Williams, an undead kid, leads the crusade for acceptance by going out for the football team; he figures they can't really hurt him. He also has an online blog that inspires undead all over the world while alerting them to the vigilantes attacking the differently biotic. Tommy is Peter's main target.

The undead become the new group to hate in this highly imaginative, darkly comedic novel. When I started reading the book, it seemed too over the top, but I quickly got hooked. Every type of bullying and harassment that exists in our schools is in this book. That alone will keep discussions going for days.

Topics for Discussion

1. How has Adam's karate training benefited him?
2. What attracts Phoebe to Tommy?
3. The dead kids are mistreated in many ways; some parents have abandoned them. How does this rejection affect all involved?

4. There are several sources of prejudices against the dead kids. Choose and explain at least two.
5. Exclusion is a form of bullying. List the ways the government excludes the differently biotic.
6. What feeds Pete's anger?
7. When Pete finds Karen alone in the woods, she seems to encourage his attack. Explain.
8. In this book, bioism is the hatred of the differently biotic. How does bioism parallel the other "isms" in our world?
9. *"Transformation always requires radical action"* (193). Give an example from your experience that proves this to be true.

Quotes for Reader Response

- "You saw it. Coach wants us to take out the dead kid." (45)
- "I'm not talking about killing *people*, man. The actual people on this list—Adam, Julie and the others—I think they deserve a good beat down for fraternizing with these monsters, but I'm not talking about killing them." (150)
- "A bioist is like a racist but hates dead folk." (165)
- "Changing the culture is a very, very difficult thing to do, even here in American." (190)
- *"Transformation always requires radical action."* (193)
- "You're all talk, Martinsburg," Coach has said. "I've heard you crow about teaching those dead kids a lesson. All you've taught them so far is a lesson in how big a coward you are." (222)
- "This happens all the time, Zombies are getting . . . murdered . . . all over the country and it . . . rarely . . . makes the news." (272)
- "Every action has consequences." (284)
- Phoebe tried to imagine the pain that the Talbots were feeling. To lose their only child, not once, but twice—how could they bear it? (293)
- "When people die, you always are going to wonder what they went through, you know. You wonder what they were thinking. If they think that you let them down." (298)

ANNOTATED BIBLIOGRAPHY

Some books are appropriate for other levels; I = intermediate grades, M = middle school, H = high school. Books discussed at length elsewhere in this text are noted parenthetically.

Picture Books

All Families Are Special by Norma Simon, illustrated by Teresa Flavin. Morton Grove, IL: Albert Whitman, 2003. After Mrs. Mack announces she will soon be a grandmother, she and the students talk about their families. They realize there are many different types of families.

All Kinds of Children by Norma Simon, illustrated by Diane Paterson. Morton Grove, IL: Albert Whitman, 1999. Children all over the world have things in common, from having belly buttons to wearing clothes to holding onto special things. Children are more alike than different.

Crickwing by Janell Cannon. New York: Harcourt, 2000. Because Crickwing has a broken wing and can't move very fast, he has to find other ways to protect himself. His artistic talents help him distract his attackers and make friends with the leaf-cutting ants.

The Family Book by Todd Parr. New York: Little, Brown, 2003. Using human and animal families displayed through colorful graphics, Parr writes about ways families are different and alike.

First Day in Grapes by L. King Pérez, illustrated by Robert Casilla. New York: Harcourt 2000. Chico and his family move when the fruit picking begins. His first day at his new school is his father's first day in grapes. (See page 30.)

Igor, the Bird Who Couldn't Sing by Stoski Kitamura. New York: Farrar, Straus and Giroux, 2005. Igor loves to sing, but no one appreciates his singing; even after he takes lessons to improve, others still booed. So he moves far away and sings alone until he finds a friend.

Is It Because? by Tony Ross. Hauppauge, NY: Barron's Educational Series, 2005. Questions plague the narrator as he tries to figure out why Wally Wormhead bullies him.

It's Okay to Be Different by Todd Parr. New York: Little, Brown, 2001. Using human and animal families displayed through colorful graphics, Parr shows ways that being different is okay.

Jag by LeAnn Rimes, illustrated by Richard Bernal. New York: Byron Preiss, 2003. Jag has to start school with all the other jaguars, but she thinks they will laugh at her because of her fear of the water. And they do.

Jungle Drums by Graeme Base. New York: Harry N. Abrams, 2004. Everyone knows warthogs get the least respect because they are not as cool as the other animals, until Ngiri, the smallest warthog in all of Africa, plays the magic drums.

Lissy's Friends by Grace Lin. New York: Viking, 2007. Lissy, the shy new girl at school, is ignored until she creates some paper origami friends to keep her company. Soon the other children want to learn how to do origami.

My Name Is Bilal by Asma Mobin-Uddin, illustrated by Barbara Kiwak. Honesdale, PA: Boyds Mills Press, 2005. Bilal and his sister Ayesha move to a new school where they are harassed because they are Muslim. (See chapter 6, "The 'Isms,'" page 102.)

Nobody Knew What to Do: A Story about Bullying by Becky Ray McCain, illustrated by Todd Leonardo. Morton Grove, IL: Albert Whitman, 2001. The narrator tells what happens when the new student, Ray, was bullied and nobody knew how to help him.

No More Bullies by Susan Hood, illustrated by Cary Pillo. New York: Scholastic, 2004. Ben, the bully, is the one who is different—he is HUGE. Not until Anne smiles at him and says "hi" does anyone believe Ben can be fun.

Pinduli by Janell Cannon. New York: Harcourt, 2004. Pinduli, a young striped hyena, suffers the attitudes of those animals that feel superior over him.

The Recess Queen by Alexis O'Neill, illustrated by Laura Huliske-Beith. New York: Scholastic, 2002. Mean Jean rules the playground until teeny-tiny Katie Sue shows up. Before she can learn Mean Jean's playground rules, Katie Sue offers friendship.

Stand Tall, Molly Lou Melon by Patty Lovell, illustrated by David Catrow. New York: G. P. Putnam's Sons, 2001. Molly

Lou is the tiniest child ever, but her grandmother taught her to believe in herself. When she transfers to a new school, this giant-sized spirit makes friends with everyone, even the school bully.

Trouble for Trudy by Terry Slater, illustrated by Sally Springer. New York: Scholastic, 2007. Other kids seem to avoid Trudy and her orange hair, thick round glasses, and unique outfits—except Annie. But after they become best friends, Annie is afraid of Trudy's bullies. The book ends with the question, "What would you do if a bully was picking on your friend?" A teacher guide is on the back cover. (See page 31.)

Ugly Duckling by Hans Christian Andersen. This bully book has been a part of all of our childhoods. It is time to reread it with a new awareness. Pick any edition.

Veronica on Petunia's Farm by Roger Duvoisin. New York: Alfred A. Knopf, 2008 (previously published 1962, 1990). Veronica is a very happy hippo, but the other animals on Mr. Pumpkin's farm do not think she belongs there. (See page 32.)

Wings by Christopher Myers. New York: Scholastic, 2000. Everyone thinks Ikarus Jackson's wings are ugly except for one quiet girl who finds her voice to tell Ikarus his wings are beautiful.

Yes We Can by Sam McBratney, illustrated by Charles Fuge. New York: HarperCollins, 2006. Little Roo, Country Mouse, and Quacker Duck have a great time in the fall leaves until Little Roo starts showing off what he can do and laughs at the others when they can't. Little Roo's mother explains that no one likes to be laughed at and suggests they admire the special talents they each have.

Yoon and the Jade Bracelet by Helen Recorvits, illustrated by Gabi Swiatkowska. New York: Farrar, Straus and Giroux, 2008. New from Korea, Yoon loans her jade bracelet to an older girl so she will jump rope with her. (See page 33.)

Intermediate

Amy Hodgepodge #1: All Mixed Up! by Kim Wayans and Kevin Knotts, illustrated by Soo Jeong. New York: Grosset and Dunlap, 2008. After being homeschooled by her family, Amy Hodges enters fourth grade at Emerson Charter School. Not only is she new, she is part black, part white, part Japanese, and part Korean. Luckily she finds a lunch table filled with kids who are just as diverse as she. The bullying in this book is secondary to the acceptance displayed for diversity. *Amy Hodgepodge #2: Happy Birthday to Me* is the next book in the series.

Blue Jasmine by Kashmira Sheth. New York: Hyperion Books, 2004. Seema and her family move to Iowa City from a small town in India where she was one of the popular girls, but in the USA she is the outsider.

Dexter the Tough by Margaret Peterson Haddix, illustrated by Mark Elliott. New York: Simon and Schuster, 2007. Dexter's first day in the fourth grade is in a new school, and when everything goes wrong he takes it out on a kid (Robin) who is crying in the bathroom. The rest of the book unravels Dexter's anger and Robin's tears and leads them to a friendship.

Drita, My Homegirl by Jenny Lombard. New York: Puffin Books, 2006. When Drita from Kosovo and Maxie from New York City meet on Drita's first day at school, they never thought they would have anything in common. (See page 34.)

Emma-Jean Lazarus Fell Out of a Tree by Lauren Tarshis. New York: Dial Books, 2007. Seventh grader Emma-Jean looks at everything from a purely logical point of view, including Laura Gilroy, the queen bee who gets everything she wants. Emma-Jean, without anger or fear, approaches this imbalance as a science project. (M)

Feathers by Jacqueline Woodson. New York: G. P. Putnam's Sons, 2007. In January of 1971, Frannie's sixth grade class gains a new student who looks white but says he is not. The other kids think he looks like Jesus—but Trevor hates him the first time he sees him. (M) (See page 103.)

The Gold-Threaded Dress by Carolyn Marsden. Cambridge, MA: Candlewick Press, 2002. Although Oy is from Thailand, the students in her fourth grade class call her Chinita, Spanish for little Chinese. What she wants most is to be accepted by Lilianda and invited to her clubhouse, and if Oy brings her traditional Thai dress to school that might happen.

Home, and Other Big, Fat Lies by Jill Wolfson. New York: Henry Holt, 2006. Having lived through eleven foster assignments,

Whitney never expects to be accepted, but in a little town in northern California things just might change. (See page 36.)

Loser by Jerry Spinelli. New York: HarperCollins, 2002. Zinkoff, from first grade through sixth grade, is a loser by everyone else's standards, but he's much too busy and excited about life to even notice people making fun of him. (M)

Medusa Jones by Ross Collins. New York: Arthur A. Levine, 2008. Medusa Jones; her three-headed dog, Cerberus; and her two friends—Chiron, a centaur, and Mino, the Minotaur—are harassed by the beautiful but snobby Perseus, Cassandra, and Thesues. In this fun mixture of mythology and contemporary time, being different still makes one an easy target for bullying. (M)

Minn and Jake by Janet S. Wong, illustrated by Genevieve Coté. New York: Frances Foster Books, 2003. Minn has always lived in Santa Brunelle and is the tallest person in the fifth grade. Jake, who just moved from Los Angeles, is the shortest boy she's ever seen, and just maybe they can be friends. Novel in verse.

Pa Lia's First Day by Michelle Edwards. New York: Harcourt, 2001 (originally published 1999). On her first day of second grade, Pa Lia doesn't want to be new so badly that it takes her forever to get to school. By the front door she meets Calliope who introduces her to Howardina, and at the end of the day she doesn't feel new any more.

Playground Bully by Thornton Jones and Debbie Dadey, illustrated by Amy Wummer. New York: Scholastic, 2001. Jack the Wonder Dog has a big bark, so big that his human, Maggie, decides Jack needs to go to school. There the Doberman bully, Sweetcakes, rules the yard.

Quit It by Marcia Byalick. New York: Delacorte Press, 2002. Recently diagnosed with Tourette's syndrome, Carrie enters the seventh grade with a new feeling of being different. (M)

Vive La Paris by Esmé Raji Codell. New York: Hyperion Books, 2006. Fifth grader Paris has four older brothers but only Michael gets physically bullied by Tanaeja, a girl in Paris's class. But Michael chooses to follow Martin Luther King's ways to handle her, while Paris befriends Mrs. Rosen, a Jewish neighbor with a fascinating but painful past. Many World War II references.

Middle School

Buddha Boy by Kathe Koja. New York: Frances Foster Books, 2003. When Jensen, with a shaven head, kind smile, and Buddhist ways, enrolls in wealthy Edward Rucher High School, Justin surprises himself by befriending this weird new kid. (H)

Can't Get There from Here by Todd Strasser. New York: Simon and Schuster, 2004. The painful stories of several homeless teenagers living (and dying) on the streets of New York City, all looking for a place to belong. (H)

Chess Rumble by G. Neri, illustrated by Jesse Joshua Watson. New York: Lee and Low, 2007. Angry over his sister's death and being bullied, Marcus eventually finds a way to channel his anger and calculate his way through problems by playing chess. (H)

Deliver Us from Normal by Kate Klise. New York: Scholastic, 2005. Eleven years old, friendless, and poor, Charles Harrisong feels emotions more deeply than most, particularly the pain of being bullied. He yearns for deliverance and for normalcy, but it is only after his sister's humiliation during her campaign for seventh grade class president that his hopes appear to be realized. (I)

Drowning Anna by Sue Mayfield. New York: Hyperion Books, 2002. Bullying can happen to anyone, and it does to thirteen-year-old Anna Goldsmith, who was a strong, independent, and socially mature young woman when she transferred into her new school, where Hayley used her and then discarded her without any explanation. Told in flashbacks after Anna has tried to kill herself, this book weaves together Anna's journal, her mother's bedside hospital watch, and the reflections of her friend, Melanie. (H)

Egghead by Caroline Pignat. Calgary: Red Deer Press, 2008. Will, the target; Kate, the bystander; and Devan, the bully's thug, find a way to become friends. (See page 39.)

Fade to Black by Alex Flinn. New York: HarperCollins, 2005. After Alex is attacked late one night in his truck, he starts to wonder if it is because he is HIV positive. The attacker could have been Clinton, who has a history of harassing Alex because of his fear of AIDS. (H)

Football Genius by Tim Green. New York: HarperCollins, 2007. Twelve-year-old Troy White has an extraordinary talent to predict an opponent's play before it happens on the football field. When his mother gets a public relations job with the Atlanta Falcons, Troy sees how his talent can help his favorite professional team and show up Jamie Renfro, the bully quarterback of his school's football team.

Funny Little Monkey by Andrew Auseon. New York: Harcourt, 2006. Arty Moore is four foot two, suffering from Growth Hormone Deficiency Syndrome, and his twin brother Kurt is six foot three. They seem to hate each other. In their competitive sibling rivalry, Arty lashes out verbally and Kurt physically. Arty connects with Kerouac, leader of an underground organization of outcasts, and gets him to go after his brother. (H)

Getting in the Game by Dawn FitzGerald. New Milford, CT: Roaring Brook Press, 2005. Feisty seventh grader Joanna Giordano fights to get on the boy's hockey team, while her grandfather is getting stranger, her father is getting more out of control, and her best friend, Ben, is ignoring her.

Impossible Things by Robin Stevenson. Victoria: Canada: Orca Book Publishers, 2008. Cassidy Silver finds herself friendless until Victoria moves in and helps change the dynamics created by the meanest girls in the class. Even her genius of a younger brother learns how to escape from the constant torment of a bully. (I)

Losers by Matthue Roth. New York: Push, 2008. Jupiter Jason Glazer and his parents left Russia seven years ago and now live in an empty warehouse outside Philadelphia. Now in junior high, Jupiter wants to avoid the insane bully Bates and find a way to fit in. For him, the first step is to lose his accent. (H)

Mia the Meek by Eileen Boggess. Baltimore: Bancroft Press, 2006. Mia enters her ninth grade year vowing to get rid of her childhood nickname of Mia the Meek. With a little push from her friend, Mia runs for class president against Cassie Foster, the most popular girl in school. (I)

Missing Matthew by Kristyn Dunnon. Calgary: Red Deer Press, 2003. When sixth grader Matthew Stein disappears, people think he was kidnapped. Winifred "Freddie" Zorn, her sister Jelly Bean, and their friend Weasel Peterson join the search and find Matt hiding in an old root cellar near the cemetery.

Before Matt moved to town, his mother had died, and when Bobby Hickmott started harassing him, Matthew couldn't take any more. (I)

No Castles Here by A. C. E. Bauer. New York: Random House, 2007. Augie Boretski is one of two white kids in his sixth grade class, and the other one torments him. But Junior Choir, a Big Brother, an ice storm, and a fantasy book change his world. (See page 41.)

On the Fringe edited by Donald R. Gallo. New York: Dial Books, 2001. Eleven original short stories by Joan Bauer, Chris Crutcher, Jack Gantos, Angela Johnson, Ron Koertge, Will Weaver, and others, focus on the experiences of teenage outsiders struggling with peer pressure, conformity, personal identity, popularity, and harassment. (H)

Owning It: Stories about Teens with Disabilities edited by Donald R. Gallo. Cambridge: Candlewick, 2008. In this original collection of ten stories by Chris Crutcher, Gail Giles, Kathleen Jeffrie Johnson, René Saldaña Jr., Brenda Woods, and others, teens with ADD, cancer, brain damage, asthma, Tourette's syndrome, and other disabilities face their problems with courage, humor, and defiance. (H)

The Plain Janes by Cecil Castellucci and Jim Rugg. New York: MINX/DC Comics, 2007. After experiencing a terrorist attack in Metro City, Jane and her family move away from the city where she will attend Buzz Aldrin High School. Wisely avoiding the "cool girls," she decides to sit at a lunch table with three loners, Jayne, Jane, and Polly Jane, whom she unites in an underground art lovers' group.

Queen of the Toilet Bowl by Frieda Wishinsky. Victoria, BC: Orca Soundings, 2005. Renata and her family left Brazil after her father died. Now in the United States, Renata works hard to be invisible in her elite school so nobody will discover her mother supports them by cleaning houses. But queen bee Liz finds out and floods the Internet with photos of Renata's mother with her head in a toilet bowl. The school deals with the situation immediately, and there is much verbal support for Renata's courage and horror about the "Internet bullying." (I)

The Revealers by Doug Wilhelm. New York: Farrar, Straus and Giroux, 2003. Russell, Elliot, and Catalina have nowhere to go for help against the harassment each is enduring, until they band together and post their experiences on the school's KidNet.

Schooled by Gordon Korman. New York: Hyperion Books, 2007. After growing up completely isolated in a hippie commune, Cap Anderson is forced into the real world when his grandmother is hospitalized with a broken hip. He soon becomes the target of the big man on campus. (H)

The Secret Blog of Raisin Rodriguez by Judy Goldschmidt. New York: Penguin, 2005. Raisin and her little sister move from Los Angeles to Philadelphia after their mom remarries. As she tries to fit in with the most popular seventh grade girls, Raisin has one hilarious adventure after another. She writes all them up in her blog, and of course, it accidentally gets spread throughout the entire school.

The Skin I'm In by Sharon G. Flake. New York: Jump at the Sun, 2000. Because Maleeka has dark-black skin and Miss Saunders, the new English teacher, has a white mark over half her face, mean-spirited Charlese targets them both. (I)

Standing against the Wind by Traci L. Jones. New York: Farrar, Straus and Giroux, 2006. Patrice Williams's southern ways are no match for the tough kids in her new Chicago middle school, where she gets called Puffy because of her unruly hair, but Monty sees more in her. The two start a friendship that will help them not only survive but also flourish.

Stargirl by Jerry Spinelli. New York: Random House, 2000. A new student named Stargirl celebrates her uniqueness in eccentric ways that at first enchant the students of Mica High School, but soon the same uniqueness makes her an outsider. (H)

This Is What I Did by Ann Dee Ellis. New York: Little, Brown, 2007. Logan wasn't popular at his old school, but he wasn't a target like at his new middle school where he carries around a guilt-filled secret that keeps him from fighting back.

High School

Alt Ed by Catherine Atkins. New York: G. P. Putnam's Sons, 2003. Ninth grader Susan Calloway has gained weight since her mother died, and though nearly invisible at school, she has managed to be assigned to a suspension alternative with five other students. One is Kale, the biggest bully in school, and another is Brendan, who is perceived to be gay and Kale's main target.

The Brimstone Journals by Ron Koertge. Cambridge, MA: Candlewick Press, 2001. Poetic narratives from the point of view of fifteen students expose the anger, hate, and longings in a suburban high school that lead to an explosive situation.

Defect by Will Weaver. New York: Farrar, Straus and Giroux, 2007. Born with facial deformities, David is an easy target at school; but no one knows the secret that really makes David feel defective: he has an extra flap of skin between his arms and his sides. (M) (See chapter 4, page 71.)

Evolution, Me & Other Freaks of Nature by Robin Brande. New York: Alfred A. Knopf, 2007. Mena Reese enters ninth grade ostracized by all her former Christian friends because she could not support their harassment of a perceived-to-be-gay student, Danny Pierce, who has moved away. This year's conflict is the evolution versus intelligent design debate, and the complications keep multiplying. (M)

The Fold by An Na, New York: G. P. Putnam's Sons, 2008. Joyce, Korean-American, is a senior in high school and concerned about her Asian look. Her best friend convinces Joyce to glue her eyelids to get "the fold effect" before going to a party. Once there, Joyce feels like part of the in-crowd and starts to consider her aunt's offer to pay for eyelid surgery so Joyce can look more "American." (M)

Gamer Girl by Mari Mancusi. New York: Dutton Children's Books, 2008. When 16-year-old Maddy is bullied by a group of elite students in her new school, she gains self-confidence playing the virtual role of a princess with magical powers in an online fantasy game, starts a manga club, and falls in love with her virtual partner. (M)

Geek Magnet by Kieran Scott. New York: G. P. Putnam's Sons, 2008. Drama abounds around the high school production of *Grease*, especially for stage manager KJ, who tries to deal with everyone—her alcoholic father, her supreme jock boyfriend, the entire cast of drama geeks, and Tama, queen of the popular crowd.

Generation Dead by Daniel Waters. New York: Hyperion Books, 2008. Adam Layman, the biggest guy on the football team, and Phoebe Kindall, his best friend and goth-girl neighbor, approach their senior year with trepidation as the number of dead kids attending keeps growing. Now, Tommy Williams, a dead kid, has even tried out for football but the head coach has put out a hit on him! The prejudice in the school and community parallels all the real life prejudice that exists against minorities. (See page 43.)

Honk If You Hate Me by Deborah Halverson. New York: Delacorte, 2007. Sixteen-year-old Monalisa Kent and her best friend Glen were pulled out of a burning factory when she was six. Ten years later Monalisa believes most of the town still blames her for starting the fire.

In the Garage by Alma Fullerton. Calgary: Red Deer Press, 2006. BJ stands at Alex's funeral trying to reconstruct how they got to this point. Both harassed, she for a deforming birthmark on one side of her face, he for homophobic rumors confirmed by the exposure of his private journal, the story is told through BJ's flashbacks and Alex's poetry. (M) (See chapter 7, page 138.)

I Was a Non-Blonde Cheerleader by Kieran Scott. New York: G. P. Putnam's Sons, 2005. Annisa moved to Sand Dune, Florida, and is the only brunette at school. When two cheerleaders get kicked off the team for alcohol use, Annisa tries out, not realizing the rest of the squad believe Annisa snitched on those two.

Jimi & Me by Jaime Adoff. New York: Hyperion Books for Children, 2005. Biracial eighth grader Keith James and his mother attempt to deal with the death of his beloved father by moving to Hollow Hills, Ohio. In his mourning, Keith dresses in the Jimi Hendrix–era clothing his father left him. That plus his friendship with Veronica, a white girl, makes him a target at his new school. Novel in verse.

The Last Exit to Normal by Michael Harmon. New York: Alfred A. Knopf. 2008. Ben Campbell, at fourteen, had a pretty normal life until his father announced he is gay, his mother leaves the family, and his father's new partner moves in. At seventeen, Ben's acting out moves the family from Spokane to Montana, where Ben meets Ron Jamison, the most troubled and violent kid in town.

My Time As Caz Hazard by Tanya Lloyd Kyi. Victoria: Orca Soundings, 2004. Caz Hazard gets transferred to a new high school when her parents separate. Placed in an LD class, she meets Amanda, who acts out viciously, Rob, the silent one, and Dorie, the quiet, oddly dressed, and most harassed even by Amanda and Caz. When Dorie commits suicide. Caz realizes how cruel Dorie had been.

Nailed by Patrick Jones. New York: Walker Books, 2006. Bret Hendricks will not conform. That gets him a girlfriend, but also gets him in trouble at school and with his dad, who understands him more than Bret ever imagined.

. . . *Or Not!* by Brian Mandabach. Woodbury. MN: Flux. 2007. Cassie Sullivan—bright, sensitive and wise beyond her fourteen years—stands up for her anti-war beliefs in a conservative Christian community filled with right wing Americans, Her school days are hell with the other students harassing her verbally and stuffing vicious notes into her locker, but she finds solace in her journal writing and the beauty around the family's cabin in the mountains. (M)

Pool Boy by Michael Simmons. Brookfield, CT: Roaring Brook, 2003. Brett Gerson hangs with the cool crowd and makes fun of the "different kids." He seems to have everything a fifteen-year-old could wish for, plus the promise of a new car when he gets his license, but then his dad goes to jail for insider trading; suddenly Brett is the different one. He gets a job cleaning pools and slowly works through the elitist attitudes he used to feel he was allowed. (M)

Quaking by Kathryn Erskine. New York: Philomel Books. 2007. Matt is a foster kid who tries to go unnoticed in her new school by the vicious school bully, Rat, who seeks her out, along with the peaceful Quaker family she lives with.

Responsible by Darlene Ryan. Victoria: Orca Book Publishers, 2007. Kevin Frasier and Erin Tennant each chooses a different way to deal with the vicious bully Nick, but all paths intersect in this realistic portrayal of the costs—and benefits—of doing the right thing.

Stoner & Spaz by Ron Koertge. Cambridge, MA: Candlewick Press, 2002. When Ben, a sixteen-year-old cerebral palsy victim and loner, teams up with drugged, tattooed, rebellious Colleen, his life is changed forever.

Strays by Ron Koertge. Cambridge: Candlewick, 2007. Ted, a 16-year-old foster kid with a sad history, tries to make his way with two foster "brothers" in a house with strange "parents" and a school full of delinquent kids. (M)

Sweethearts by Sara Zarr. New York: Little, Brown, 2008. Jennifer Harris and Cameron Quick survived their childhood because they had each other; but in third grade, Cameron and his family move away. Nine years later, Jennifer—now Jenna—has transformed herself and is part of the popular circle. Then Cameron Quick comes home, the one person who knows everything about her and still loves her. (M)

The Throwaway Piece by Jo Ann Yolanda Hernandez. Houston: Arte Publico Press, 2006. After years of taking care of her alcoholic mother, Jewel, a gifted loner, finds herself a "state kid" when her mother abandons her for a string of loser boyfriends. Jewel finds herself on a self-destructive path for survival.

Total Constant Order by Crissa-Jean Chappell. New York: HarperCollins, 2007. Tap, tap, tap may ward off the bad luck for Fin, but it doesn't stop the unwanted voices in her head, the isolation of ninth grade in a new city, the harassment by the alpha female in the alpha clique, or her parents' divorce. Fin's eventual friendship with Thayer Pinsky and her developing understanding that her need for the rituals is caused by an obsessive compulsive disorder help her to bring a healthier order to her life.

4

Body Image

Say the words "body image" to a teenager and you may get a multitude of reactions—but you will get a reaction. The teenage years are all about the body: how to dress it up, dress it down, undress it, hide it, or flaunt it. And of course, everyone is judging what is done to it—and talking about it.

Teens are controlled by the strange, incredible, delightful, embarrassing things their bodies do. It sprouts hair in some places and pimples in others. As the body changes from moment to moment, it overrides common sense. Few teenagers are happy with their bodies.

Self-concept links to body image through appearance—curly hair, straight hair, big nose, big ears, tiny eyes, flat chest, full chest, pecs, no pecs, pencil-thin legs, stumpy legs, big butt, no butt—and genes we get from our heritage: skin color, papa's cleft chin, mom's hips. Later there will be blood pressure problems, high cholesterol, and hair loss. Our body image never stops changing.

The physical image we have of ourselves, the image we see in the mirror, and the image we believe others see are rarely the same. Harassment based on body image begins in the judgment of others and it alters our self-esteem.

When our national consciousness was first raised about sexual harassment, the term "hostile environment" came into usage to describe an environment with a prevailing attitude that labels or demeans a particular group of people. At that time it applied to women; I believe that now our culture is a hostile environment for overweight people. The media industry and the fashion world contribute to a belief that anyone who is overweight deserves to be humiliated. Almost everywhere in this country it is acceptable to ridicule people who do not fit the thin ideal. We are all defined by our inches instead of our souls—and there isn't any place worse than schools, from kindergarten through high school, for this kind of harassment.

In this chapter, all of the books deal with body image, and though many things can make up a person's image of his or her body, teens are most concerned with fitting the popular model. It isn't always about the scale; sometimes it is about having big ears like Otis, the dog and main character in *Dog Eared* by Amanda Harvey, or Georgie, the dwarf in *The Thing about Georgie* by Lisa Graff; or a hook nose like Cameron Beekman, who chooses to have rhinoplasty to change the family nose that her sister decides to keep in *Fix* by Leslie Margolis, which discusses the popularity of cosmetic surgery and the availability of body makeovers. In *Big Fat Manifesto* by Susan Vaught, Jamie Carcaterra turns the rage she feels for society and herself into a column in the school newspaper and eventually draws national attention.

Accepting one's personal body image may not be easy. Reading about others who have the same problems will help young people feel less lonely. These books start a discussion that will prevent this hostile environment from ruining any more lives.

FOCUS BOOKS

Picture Books

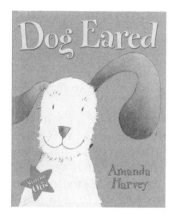

Dog Eared by Amanda Harvey. New York: Doubleday Books, 2002.

My ears were quite large. Huge, in fact.

Otis had never thought about his ears until one day, when he and Lucy, his human, are on their way home from the park, a big dog says, "Out of my way, Big Ears!" After checking his image in a store window, he becomes self-conscious about his ears. It isn't until Lucy comes downstairs to snuggle with him and curls his ears around her that Otis feels better.

Topics for Discussion

1. How many of you have pets?
2. What do you like best about your pet?
3. Is anything wrong with Otis's ears?
4. After the bully dog says that to Otis, how does Otis's feelings about himself change?
5. Why does doubt creep into Otis's mind?
6. What helps Otis realize his ears are just right?

Quotes for Reader Response

- But doubt crept into my mind.
- I couldn't eat my treats.
- Should I tie them in a bow?
- "I love your large, silky, fabulous ears."
- I don't think so!

I Get So Hungry by Bebe Moore Campbell, illustrated by Amy Bates. New York: Penguin, 2008.

> *Potato chips always make me feel better when I'm sad.*

Nikki feels sad when Arnold calls her names—like Supersize and Nikki Thicky—and when she is sad, she sneaks snacks. The doctor tells her mom, "No more junk food!" But mom likes it even more than Nikki. After Mrs. Patterson returns from being sick, Nikki notices that her clothes are looser and that she walks around the school every morning.

Nikki joins Mrs. Patterson on the early walks and gets her mom
to walk with her on weekends.

Topics for Discussion

1. Why does Arnold think he can call Nikki names?
2. How does Nikki feel when Arnold calls her names?
3. How do you feel when someone calls you names?
4. Do you have a favorite food that you sometimes just can't
   stop eating? What is your favorite food?
5. Exercise is an important way to stay healthy. What do you
   do for exercise?
6. When people tease your friend, what can you do to support
   your friend?

Quotes for Reader Response

- Once I start eating, it's hard to stop.
- When we reach our block, I can hear the doughnuts calling.
  Nikki, come taste me, Nikki, please eat me.
- But I don't want to be so big anymore.
- "My New Year's resolution is to eat less and exercise
  more."
- "Hey, Arnold, open your eyes. The only thing fat around
  here is your mouth!" Keisha and Sarah say.

Intermediate

Nothing's Fair in Fifth Grade by Barthe DeClements. New
York: Puffin Books, 2009 (originally published 1990).

> *I knew everyone hated having Elsie in our room.* (5)

Jennifer tells the story of what happens when Elsie Edwards joins
her fifth grade class. Elsie's mother brings her to the classroom
and shares with Mrs. Hanson that Elsie is on a very restricted diet
and cannot eat anything except what is in her lunch box. Mrs.
Edwards says this loudly enough for the whole class to hear. Elsie
keeps her eyes on the floor, while everyone in the class looks at
her immense body. The unkind comments start immediately.

At lunch, the carrot, broth, and pear in her lunch box are just not enough, and Elsie asks other kids if she can have some of their lunches. Some share, some don't. Some call her names, and some only think them. Eventually Jennifer learns that Elsie's mother does not treat Elsie very kindly and is thinking of sending her to a boarding school to get rid of her. More students start to look past her size and become Elsie's friends.

I like this story because everyone changes, Elsie loses weight, the students drop their judgments of overweight people, and even Elsie's mother decides not to send her away for school, plus Jennifer's mom is a solid role model from the beginning. The problems that face an overweight child or a child new to the school are difficult, but for one child to have both of these seems to multiply her difficulties every day. Perhaps the oldest childhood rhyme is "Fatty, fatty two-by-four . . ." Harassment of overweight people is not a new happening.

Topics for Discussion

1. How do the students react when Elsie joins their class?
2. List three things that explain how Elsie's mother treats her.
3. Why does Elsie eat so much?
4. Does everyone in the class really hate Elsie or do they just like to make fun of her? Is there a difference between the two?
5. How does Elsie repay the money she has stolen?
6. What helps Elsie lose weight?
7. Could you hate someone just because that person was really tall? Or really short? Why is it okay to hate someone who is overweight?

Quotes for Reader Response

- "But I get so hungry," Elsie whimpered. She sneaked a look around the room. I didn't feel sorry for her. I was glad she was getting it. She was so gross. (7)
- While I watched Mother cut up the potatoes, I told her about Elsie. "I wonder why she eats so much," Mother said. I thought that was a strange question. Didn't Elsie eat because she was hungry? (8–9)
- The boys started calling Elsie "Scrounge." And she was the classroom reject. (12)
- "I don't think [my mother] wants anyone to know I belong to her. I'm too fat, I guess." (14)
- "Look at me, Lester, Jack." The boys looked at [Mr. Marshall]. "If you don't like people to laugh at you, then don't you make fun of other people." (46)
- I had never thought of Elsie as a human being. Just a fat girl. (49)
- The more I knew Elsie the more I forgot she was fat. She had the prettiest teeth when she smiled, which wasn't very often. (75)

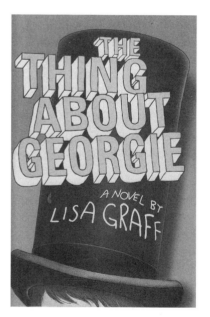

The Thing about Georgie by Lisa Graff. New York: Laura Geringer Books, 2006.

And as often as he pushed his ugliest thought to the back of his head, it always managed to find its way out again. (107–8)

Everyone else in his fourth grade class keeps growing taller while Georgie Bishop stays steady at forty-two inches, but with his terrific parents and his best friend Andy Moretti, even bully Jeanie "the Meanie" Wallace can't upset him too much. Then Georgie's parents tell him he will soon have a little brother or sister; Andy becomes super friends with Russ and wants him to help with their dog walking business; and Georgie has to partner with Jeanie for his president's report. It just isn't fair! Life is hard enough as a dwarf! He has been replaced as a best friend and soon will be replaced at home by Baby Godzilla who will be taller than Georgie much too quickly.

Georgie and Jeanie work on their Abraham Lincoln project in class, and one day after school they work at her house where Georgie sees how her older brothers call her names and make fun of her. When Mr. Meyers tells the class they will have a class play about the presidents and they will need to sign up, Georgie doesn't want to be in the play. But Jeanie secretly signs him up to be Abraham Lincoln, and he gets the part. Jeanie helps him create a costume, complete with coffee-can stilts and ruler-arm extensions, a long coat, a tall hat, and a beard. The night of the performance, he steals the show. On the way home he asks his mom and dad the really tough questions about him and the baby.

Throughout the book, there is the bonus of another voice asking the reader to do some simple tasks, like raising your right arm over your head and touching your left ear. It is a simple task most of us can do easily, but the voice explains that Georgie can't. That voice belongs to Jeanie; maybe she isn't so mean after all.

Topics for Discussion

1. List all the ways Georgie's dwarfism limits him.
2. How do you limit yourself?
3. How have others tried to help Georgie?
4. "Okay, here's what I need you to do. Figure out what your thing is, and then write it down on that piece if paper." (44)
5. Why do people stare when they see someone who is different?
6. What's the best way to make a bully understand the impact of his or her actions?
7. List all the names that Jeanie the Meanie calls Georgie.
8. What is an appropriate consequence for Jeanie's name-calling?
9. Georgie is very worried about the baby. What are two of his fears?

Quotes for Reader Response

- *Only you complete our song.* (18)
- If his parents wanted to have another kid, a perfectly normal-looking, *nice and healthy* one, great. He didn't care. (30)
- No one knew it, but long ago Georgie had glued a tape measure to the back wall of his closet. Every year on his birthday Georgie marked how tall he was. (47)
- There was Russ and Andy doing everything together perfectly, and there was Georgie looking like a moron. (66)
- "Why, are you gonna look up books about shrimpazoids like you?" (88)
- After the play Georgie changed back into his regular clothes, but somehow he felt taller than normal, as though a little bit of coffee were still stuck to the bottoms of his shoes. (204)
- "Okay. Um . . ." He cleared his throat again. "Were you disappointed that I—" He broke off, "I mean . . . would you love me more if I played the violin?" (208)

Middle School

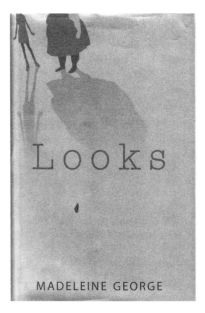

Looks by Madeleine George. New York: Viking, 2008.

> *I understand that adolescence is complicated. Physically, yes, but more than anything else adolescence is ethically complicated.* (59)

Meghan Ball is an invisible fat girl. That may seem impossible, but both of these conditions help her to cope. Life used to be easier when she had her friends Cara Roy and James Barlett, but they dropped her in seventh grade when they remade themselves to be popular. In ninth grade she sees Aimee Zorn, the thin, angular, defiant, and friendless new girl, and senses she and Aimee will be friends.

Simply being in school tortures Meghan; everyone sees the fat girl but no one acknowledges her. She has worked this invisibility to her advantage: she floats in and out of the office unseen—stopping to pick up an extra pack of hall passes and to listen to the current conflicts. In P.E. Meghan knows Mr. Cox is disgusted by her, so she tries to spare him her presence by showing up just often enough not to fail. She spends her days negotiating through the school's hostile environment.

Aimee, a poet, attends the *Photon* editorial collective meeting where they are critiquing poetry submissions. Cara Roy runs the meeting efficiently and tactfully, coaxing both praise and constructive remarks to help better the examined work. Aimee's poem about the "fat girl" impresses Cara, and she invites Aimee to her home so they can share their poetry. At school Meghan sees Aimee talking with Cara, and she feels she must warn Aimee not to trust Cara. Aimee does not listen to this strange fat girl who has never spoken to her before, but a few weeks later after Aimee realizes Cara has won the competition by plagiarizing one of Aimee's poem, she seeks out Meghan for help.

This book deals with obesity and anorexia, friendship and betrayal, isolation and survival, invisibility and courage, and it speaks to what is happening in our schools.

Topics for Discussion

1. How can Meghan be invisible when she is such a large physical presence?
2. How do others help her to be invisible?
3. Who is the greater bully, Cara or J-Bar?
4. What motivates J-Bar to bully Meghan?
5. How are J-Bar and Mr. Cox similar? Could J-Bar grow up to be just like Mr. Cox?
6. Meghan and Cara both have unhealthy coping skills. Meghan uses food. What does Cara use?
7. How do you cope with stress?
8. Who in the book offers unconditional love/acceptance?
9. What makes Mr. Handsley a better teacher than Mr. Cox?
10. Are you obesophobic?

Quotes for Reader Response

- Meghan Ball is at once the most visible and invisible person in school. (3)
- His voice oozes out of him like rancid caramel. "I want you to have my babies, Butter Ball!" (6)
- But Valley Regional High is not a humane institution. It is more like a cruel and unusual penal colony in which every inmate and every guard is punished, each according to his deepest fear. (9–10)
- Like a flash flood the image courses through Aimee's mind: the giant girl, slow as a prehistoric creature, the boys like a pack of wolves at her back, the girl's eyes behind her bangs open but seeing nothing, silvered over like the eyes of a dead fish on ice. (21)
- *My arms wrap two times / around my own ribs, / meet behind my back for a secret / handshake.* (105)
- The fat girl left alone in the world sees that every human being has a value assigned to them that they are helpless to change no matter what they do, and she sees that people trade each other like baseball cards: three cheap friends for two valuable friends, a whole group of worthless friends for one popular friend. (143–44)
- This must be how the body reacts to deception. This must be how the immune system fights off the feeling of being violated by a friend. (149)
- As long as you never open your mouth and tell other people how to treat you, they're going to treat you however they please, maybe even quite badly, and they'll take your silence as permission to do so. (218)
- "When I look at you, Ms. Ball, what I see is a lovely young woman who is bright and strong and sensitive, and so observant I can actually observe you observing sometimes." (218)
- Look at how no one looks at them as they pass. No one follows them down the hall any more, no one stops them at their lockers. No one corners them in the gym or the stairwell or the parking lot. No one notices them as they wait for the late bus or eat their lunch together on the floor in a corner. Look at the new way they've invented to be invisible. (239)

High School

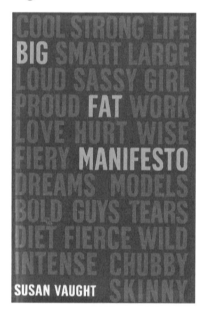

Big Fat Manifesto by Susan Vaught. New York: Bloomsbury, 2008.

Choices make ripples that never stop. (280)

High school senior Jamie D. Carcaterra, is many things: a writer, an actress, Burke's girl-friend, a strong independent thinker, and a fat girl. Guess which one the world chooses to see? So why not be the fat girl with an attitude? She makes her size the focus of her weekly column in the school's news-paper, and when Burke decides to have a bariatric procedure—gastric bypass—he gives Jamie carte blanche to write about it.

Jamie has done her research and she knows the risks involved, which are higher for blacks than whites; the potential dangers after; and the extreme limitations that must be followed. Do the risks outweigh (seriously, no pun intended) the advantages? Jamie's other two closest friends are also women with strong convictions. Freddie is an open lesbian and "Ms. Anchor" on the Garwood High cable station—and doesn't take anything from anyone. NoNo, a seemingly quiet, shy young woman, carries the conscience of the world and supports nearly all causes and cru-sades. The three of them make a formidable team.

Jamie's editor, Heath Montel, supports her column and even pushes her to go farther. After reporting on Burke's surgery, some very serious complications, and his continued weight loss, Jaime draws media attention with her column, first local and then national. Because Jamie's column challenges the fat-is-nearly-sinful attitude of the masses by exposing the surgery's ugly risks, the school administration and Burke's parents want her to stop. At the suggestion of Jamie's parents, one final column bringing Burke's success up to date is agreed upon.

Through the course of the book, Jamie and Burke change. Burke still loves her, but he now has a new body and he unconsciously looks at Jamie differently. Jamie has new questions to ask herself about the possibility of bariatric surgery and the fierce attitude she has used in her column. Sometimes she has felt like two people. And then there is Heath, who has always admired her from afar, stepping forward to hold her during her meltdowns.

Topics for Discussion

1. What drives Jamie to write the Fat Girl column?
2. Jamie, Freddie, and NoNo, incredibly close friends, are very different. What binds them together?
3. Why is NoNo such a perfect name for Nora Nostenfast?
4. Jamie has fears about Burke's surgery, some for him and some for herself. What are her fears for herself?
5. Do you think Jamie should have the surgery if her parents' medical insurance would cover it?
6. This book sheds light on discrimination against fat people. Discuss some of the scenes where that happens. Did anything reported in the book surprise you?
7. What is the worst part of being fat?
8. Why do many people believe that bariatric surgery is an easy way to lose weight? Did you learn anything new about these surgeries from reading Jamie's columns?
9. Are you obesophobic?

Quotes for Reader Response

- I haven't eaten in front of people since fifth grade, when I got tired of the staring, even from the teachers. (14)
- The women at the register give me a few more snide expressions, then ignore me. Seems like the bigger I get, the more invisible I become. Another fifty pounds, and I'll be an outright ghost. (25)
- I know white people die from it! . . . One in two hundred, and that's only counting patients who die on the table or right after they get the surgery. (45)
- And you're black, so you're *three times* more likely to die from it—and the doctors don't even know why. (46)

- Obesity surgery is *not* an easy way out of being fat. (82)
- This is what THIN is worth to Fat Boy. More than agony, more than breath, more than love, more than life. (136)
- *Do I want it?* (155)
- Sometimes I think you keep so busy, you run so hard, so none of the other shit can catch up to you. (204)
- *Primum non nocere,* First do no harm. (249)
- Fat kids aren't necessarily more likely to be depressed, but depressed kids are likely to be fat. So depression might cause fat, but fat doesn't have to cause depression. (264–65)
- Because if you believe in your causes, sooner or later you have to take risks for them. You have to behave like you believe. (286–87)

Defect by Will Weaver. New York: Farrar, Straus and Giroux, 2007.

> *Crowded together, they are a family of strangers. All of them hanging by an iron thread. All of them in this together. All of them falling. . . . David feels the burn of tears in his eyes, feels some insane kind of joy.* (59)

David has lived his fifteen years as a freak, struggling to hide his abnormalities from the world. The bullies have always been there, first through his early years with his mom in New York, and then when she couldn't take care of him through multiple foster homes in Minnesota, until he was placed with the Trotwoods.

At school, David's bug eyes, pinched face, hearing aids, and rounded back are obvious, but what no one can see is the extra flesh between David's arms and sides that he can unfurl and use like a glider to fly. After an intense showdown with Kael Grimes and his thugs, David leads them to believe he has thrown himself off Barn Bluff. When he confronts them the next day at school, the bullies are angry and suspicious and intensify the attacks. The principal decides David needs to transfer to Oak Leaf Alternative School, and though David and the Trotwoods disagree, the transfer is made. Once there, David quickly makes friends in its more welcoming environment. Cheetah, a young woman his age who has epilepsy, becomes a very special friend. Before long another student, not realizing it is David, tells of seeing someone jump off Barn Cliff and seemingly fly. The word spreads and soon the media are alerted. People surround David's home believing he is an injured angel. Dr. Ramaswamy, the first doctor who ever examined David, arrives and wants to take him to the nearby Mayo Clinic. After several tests, he and other doctors offer David a makeover that would give him a new face and remove his wings. He would be normal. David must make the decision for himself.

Topics for Discussion

1. How does the author make David's ability to fly seem scientifically possible? Did you wonder if it could be possible?
2. How do the years of keeping his abnormalities a secret affect David?
3. Why does David want to stay at Valley View High School?
4. How does David change at Oak Leaf Alternative School?
5. Why is David hesitant to trust Mr. and Mrs. Trotwood?
6. If you had an extra flap of skin like David's and could fly like he did, would you consider the surgery?
7. Does David have a defect or a gift?
8. At the end of the book, David is about to speak to the media. How will he satisfy their curiosity?

Quotes for Reader Response

- "Just because you look weird, that's no reason why you have to act weird." (3)
- "I shouldn't have to look at that freak all day." (4)

- Sometimes he thinks he knows what it's like to be a girl—the way men's eyes scan their bodies up and down as if they're newspapers with headlines to be read. (23)
- "Hey, Ugly Boy, where's your momma now!" (70)
- "Look at me. . . . There's no plainer-looking farm wife in the whole Midwest. I have a face like a potato, shoulders like an old workhorse. Don't you think I'd like to be beautiful, . . . But that's not going to happen." (79)
- The nurses gasp as one; they stumble backward. The doctor grunts as if he has been punched in the gut. "What the hell do we have here?" (103)
- "Hey, I have seen way weirder things during my seizures." (109)
- He takes Cheetah by the chin—roughly—and forces her to look closely at his face, "Would you look this way if you didn't have to?" (156)
- *Cheetah's a nice girl, but think of the chicks you could have if you looked like me.* (187)
- "What if I didn't . . . have the operation?" (197)

ANNOTATED BIBLIOGRAPHY

Some books are appropriate for other levels; I = intermediate grades, M = middle school, H = high school. Books discussed at length elsewhere in this text are noted parenthetically.

Picture Books

Betty Lou Blue by Nancy Crocker, illustrated by Boris Kulikov. New York: Dial Books, 2006. All the children tease Betty Lou and call her names because she has huge feet, but when a snowstorm blows in, only Betty Lou can carry them to safety.

Crickwing by Janell Cannon. New York: Harcourt, 2000. Because Crickwing has a broken wing and can't move very fast, he has to find other ways to protect himself. His artistic talents help him distract his attackers and make friends with the leaf-cutting ants.

Dog Eared by Amanda Harvey. New York: Doubleday Books, 2002. Otis is a hound-type dog with hound-type ears—big—

and the other dogs laugh at him, but Lucy loves to cuddle his ears and wrap them around her face. (See page 60.)

I Get So Hungry by Bebe Moore Campbell, illustrated by Amy Bates. New York: Penguin, 2008. Arnold calls Nikki names like Supersize to get a laugh from the other students. Nikki doesn't like being overweight, but she doesn't have any hope that she can change, until she sees her teacher walking everyday before and after school. (See page 61.)

It's Okay to Be Different by Todd Parr. New York: Little, Brown, 2001. Using human and animal families displayed through colorful graphics, Parr shows ways that being different is okay.

Jungle Drums by Graeme Base. New York: Harry N. Abrams, 2004. Everyone knows warthogs get the least respect because they are not as cool as the other animals, until Ngiri, the smallest warthog in all of Africa, plays the magic drums.

Little Zizi by Thierry Lenain, illustrated by Stéphane Poulin, translated by Daniel Zolinsky. El Paso: Cinco Puntos Press, 2008. While the boys are changing after swim class, Adrian sees Martin naked and announces to everyone that Martin has a little zizi. He also tells Martin that he will never be able to make babies. (See chapter 2, page 9.)

Pinduli by Janell Cannon. San Diego: Harcourt, 2004. Pinduli, a young striped hyena, suffers the attitudes of those animals that feel superior.

Intermediate

Larger-Than-Life Lara by Dandi Daley Mackall. New York: Dutton Children's Books, 2006. Laney Grafton writes a story about a few weeks in her fourth grade class when Lara Phelps, a very large girl, joins the class and Joey Gilbert starts the verbal attacks.

Medusa Jones by Ross Collins. New York: Arthur A. Levine, 2008. Medusa Jones, her three-headed dog, Cerberus, and her two friends—Chiron, a centaur, and Mino, the Minotaur—are harassed by the beautiful Perseus, Cassandra, and Thesues. In this fun mixture of mythology and contemporary time, being different still makes one an easy target for bullying. (M)

Nothing's Fair in Fifth Grade by Barthe DeClements. New York: Puffin Books, 2009 (originally published 1990). When Elsie joins Jennifer's fifth grade class, her mother makes sure everyone knows she is on a diet. Everyone makes fun of her until Jennifer learns what Elsie's life is like and they become friends. (See page 63.)

The Skin I'm In by Sharon G. Flake. New York: Jump at the Sun, 2000. Because Maleeka has dark-black skin, the other kids torment her. Miss Saunders, the new English teacher, has a white mark over half her face. Charlese doesn't let up on either of them. (M)

Stink, the Incredible Shrinking Kid by Megan McDonald, illustrated by Peter H. Reynolds. Cambridge, MA: Candlewick Press, 2006. Stink, only five feet three inches tall and the shortest kid in his second grade class, tries everything to get taller. On President's day, Stink honors President James Madison, the shortest president of the United States at five feet four inches tall.

The Thing about Georgie by Lisa Graff. New York: Laura Geringer Books, 2006. Fourth grader Georgie has lots of great things in his life, including a wonderful family and Andy who is a terrific best friend. But mean Jeanne has bullied him since kindergarten just because he is a dwarf. (See page 64.)

Middle School

Artichoke's Heart by Suzanne Supplee. New York: Dutton Children's Books, 2008. Consumed by overeater's guilt, fifteen-year-old Rosie Goode puts all her effort into searching for the magic cure for fat because no one sees past her pounds. After a sudden ten-pound weight gain over Christmas vacation, she decides she has to do something, and she does. Along the way she also learns how to talk to people, make a friend, and help her mother through treatment for Hodgkin's Disease. (H)

Beastly by Alex Flinn. New York: HarperCollins, 2007. In this modern version of *The Beauty and the Beast*, Kyle Kingbury seems to have it all—perfect looks, elite friends, and lots of money—but he lacks empathy and compassion. At a school dance he plays a particularly wicked trick on a girl who is outside his social circle, but she turns out to be a witch who gets even with an ugly spell that turns Kyle into a beast. (H)

In the Garage by Alma Fullerton. Calgary: Red Deer Press, 2006. The book opens with BJ trying to give the eulogy at Alex's funeral. They have been friends since third grade when Alex stood up to the bullies who harassed BJ about the mark on her face. The book covers the eight years between those two events. (H)

Looks by Madeleine George. New York: Viking, 2008. Ninth grader Meghan Ball, extremely overweight and yet invisible, doesn't have any friends and rarely talks at school. Aimee Zorn, thin and angular, writes raw yet sensitive poetry but only shows the world her resentment. She doesn't have any friends either, until Cara Roy. Meghan tries to warn Aimee that Cara uses people and then stays to help Aimee recover from Cara's manipulation. (H) (See page 66.)

Out of Order by Robin Stevenson. New York: Hyperion Books, 2008. A new, thinner Sophie Keller starts her sophomore year at a school in Victoria, finally able to escape the name-calling and harassment of her previous school. Cautious to make friends, Sophie meets Zelia, eccentric in attitude, clothes, and her need for fun. Sophie continues to starve herself and pretend things are fine, until she sees she has choices.

Perfect by Natasha Friend. Minneapolis: Milkweed Editions, 2004. Isabelle's father died two years ago, and after the service, someone suggested she might feel better if she ate something. She did; she ate everything on the buffet table and then threw up. Now two years later, her little sister finds her vomiting in the bathroom and calls their mom. Isabelle starts "group" and discovers the most perfect girl in the school, Ashley Barnum, is there too. (H)

Remembering Raquel by Vivian Vande Velde. New York: Harcourt, 2007. Raquel Falcone was hit by a car and killed. The story takes place at the funeral home, told through the voices of her father, her childhood friend Hayley, Raquel's blog, the driver of the car, a few witnesses, some teachers, and some students, including the girls who judged her because of her weight—but who now claim her as one of their friends. (I)

High School

Alt Ed by Catherine Atkins. New York: G. P. Putnam's Sons, 2003. Susan Callaway, an overweight, silent tenth grader, is assigned Alt Ed, an alternative-to-suspension program, for a passive aggressive attack on her main tormentor. The six students involved in this group slowly discover how interwoven their lives have become.

Big Fat Manifesto by Susan Vaught. New York: Bloomsbury, 2008. Jamie Carcaterra knows she is fat; everyone has pointed it out to her. She turns her anger into a weekly column for the school newspaper where she tries to educate others on the myths and frustrations of being fat along with the dangers of bariatric surgery that her boyfriend has elected to have done. (M) (See page 69.)

By the Time You Read This, I'll Be Dead by Julie Anne Peters. New York: Hyperion Books, 2010. Having been bullied about her weight since she was five, Daelyn finds nothing validating in life. She's attempted suicide before, but this time she's determined. At school she has started connecting with an unusual boy and an overweight girl, but it may already be too late.

Dancing in Red Shoes Will Kill You by Dorian Cirrone. New York: HarperCollins 2005. Kayla Calloway studies to be a ballet dancer but loses her chance for the solo in *Cinderella* because of her big breasts. Her ballet instructor suggests Kayla consider breast reduction surgery, and when that bit of news gets out, the whole school joins the debate. (M)

Defect by Will Weaver. New York: Farrar, Straus and Giroux, 2007. Born with facial deformities, David is an easy target at school, but no one knows the secret that really makes David feel defective. He has extra flaps of skin between his arms and his sides that enable him to fly. (M) (See page 71.)

Fat Kid Rules the World by K. L. Going. New York: G. P. Putnam's Sons, 2003. Troy, six foot one and nearly three hundred pounds, feels like the biggest slob in the world and considers suicide until he meets Curt, an emaciated guitar genius who sees Troy's potential.

Fix by Leslie Margolis. New York: Simon Pulse, 2006. Cruelly harassed about her hook nose, Cameron Beekman had rhinoplasty, moved to a new school, and remade herself into one of the gorgeous people. Her younger sister, Allie, has the same nose but a different personality; however, her parents are trying to push her into the same surgery. The book discusses the popularity of cosmetic surgery and the availability of body makeovers. (M)

The Fold by An Na. New York: G. P. Putnam's Sons, 2008. Joyce, a Korean American, is a senior in high school and concerned about her Asian look. Her best friend convinces Joyce to glue her eyelids to get "the fold effect" before going to a party; once there Joyce feels like part of the in-crowd and starts to consider her aunt's offer to pay for eyelid surgery so Joyce can look more "American." (M)

Huge by Sasha Paley. New York: Simon and Schuster, 2007. April Adams has saved up seven thousand dollars to go to Wellness Camp, aka Fat Camp, to become the person she has always dreamed of being. There she meets her roommate, Wilhelmina Hopkins, who intends to gain weight to get back at her parents for not loving her as she is.

Massive by Julia Bell. New York: Simon Pulse, 2002. Fourteen-year-old Carmen has a mom with a severe anorexia eating disorder that spills over onto Carmen as the chaos in their lives spreads.

Pretty Face by Mary Hogan. New York: HarperCollins, 2008. Hayley, a girl with curves, has issues with her body, boys, and her compulsively dieting mother, who buys Hayley a talking scale and then listens outside the door. Allowed to go to Italy for the summer, Hayley finds a simpler, less judgmental life style—and Enzo.

Sweethearts by Sara Zarr. New York: Little, Brown, 2008. Jennifer Harris and Cameron Quick survived their childhood because they had each other, but then in third grade, Cameron and his family moved away. Nine years later, Jennifer, now Jenna, has transformed—no longer overweight, mousey, timid, and with poor hygiene, she has a circle of friends and a boyfriend. Then Cameron Quick comes home, the one person who knows everything about her and still loves her. (M)

5

Cliques, Groups, and Gangs

Would you rather be nice or popular? Asking that question of most middle school students puts them in a quandary. They know the answer their parents want them to give, but the temptations and rewards of popularity are awesome. When I first awoke to this teen value, I asked a series of questions. Is being nice and being popular the same thing? Do being nice and being popular naturally go together? The response was a strong resounding—No. I asked if popular people were nice? Again, No. Are nice people popular? Not usually. Not all students feel the need to be popular over everything else, but the school culture rewards those who are. And the main, if not the only, way to be popular is to fit in with the "popular kids." If there isn't a popular clique, how would everyone define themselves? Does membership in the popular clique define success?

The most upsetting thing I have had to accept is what our young people will trade away in order to fit in. They will abandon their friends, their family, their values, and their identity to assume the identity required by the popular crowd. The healthiest of our young people can move between several different circles, feeling comfortable in each and helping others to feel the same.

In the humorous *Cliques, Phonies & Other Baloney*, Trevor Romain lists "four dorky things cliques do":

- They always travel in a group.
- They have rules.

- They have leaders who make the rules.
- They have a dress code.[1]

The one thing Romain doesn't list is that cliques exclude. That exclusivity creates its own attractiveness and power. The sense of community is devalued as the exclusivity is more highly valued. Membership is not about a common belief, interest, or talent; it is about keeping others out and flaunting it. Some of these groups feel it is their responsibility to set the standard, and that leads to group membership requirements, a screening, and an initiation—which leads to hazing. Whether the group is a sports team; the wealthy, beautiful kids; an area gang; or a girls "pink" clique, exclusion and hazing are all about power and all about harassment, and when a group bullies, they are far more powerful than when an individual bullies.

It starts young. In Marion Dane Bauer's *The Double-Digit Club*, the first girl to turn ten starts her own club for those who are ten and the first rule is they do not talk to nine-year-olds. The exclusion may only go on for that school year, but it is practice for later grades. *Poison Ivy* by Amy Goldman Koss tells of a girls' group's harassment of Ivy that started in early elementary school, and everyone watched it happen and supported it out of fear. Chela, in *The Smell of Old Lady Perfume* by Claudia Guadalupe Martinez, returns to school after her father has a heart attack and discovers her best friend has joined Camila's group and can't be friends with her anymore. *Walking Naked* by Alyssa Brugman is told by one of the insiders, Megan. Their top clique is so tight they call interventions on members who are not behaving appropriately. They all hate Perdita and follow her through the halls chanting "Freak, Freak" just loud enough for her to hear but not the teachers.

In *The Losers' Club* by John Lekich, the "haves" torment the "have-nots," who bond in weekly meetings and make Alex, the kid with cerebral palsy, their leader. *The Beckoners* by Carrie Mac gives us Zoe, new to the high school and unfortunate enough to draw the attention of Beck, leader of the Beckoners, and she wants Zoe in her gang. The initiation includes a branding with a fork. But in Gail Giles's *Shattering Glass*, Rob manipulates the other high school boys into following him—right into murder.

The basic need to belong pushes all of us to find that fit. Younger people are no different. But there is a difference between an exclusive group of people and a circle of individuals who welcome everybody. One feels good.

FOCUS BOOKS

Picture Books

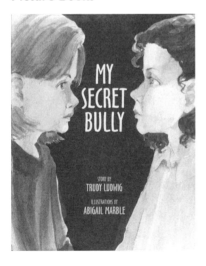

My Secret Bully by Trudy Ludwig, illustrated by Abigail Marble. Ashland, Oregon: RiverWood Books, 2004.

> *I like being around Katie when she's nice to me. But there are times when she's not. She can be just plain mean.*

Monica and Katie have been friends since they met in kindergarten, but lately Katie almost seems mean. Sometimes she whispers to other girls, and then they all giggle when she points to Monica. Other times Katie doesn't want Monica to play with anyone else. Monica starts getting a nervous stomach. Her mom suggests she and Katie talk it out, but Katie doesn't have time to talk. Monica begins to think maybe there is something wrong with her, and she gets such a bad stomach ache that she stays home from school. Her mom knows something is wrong, and when she asks, Monica tells her everything. Together they role-play what Monica can do the next time Katie acts hurtful. When she does, Monica is ready and says what she practiced with her mom.

A section at the end of the book defines relational aggression, suggests some strategies to help the targeted person, and provides some additional resources.

Topics for Discussion

1. What does Katie do that makes Monica feel left out?
2. Has anyone ever tried to make you feel left out? Explain.
3. Why do the other girls go along with Katie?
4. How does Katie try to control Monica?
5. Explain how Monica's mom helped her.
6. What does the title *My Secret Bully* mean?

Quotes for Reader Response

- "Oh nothing, Mon-ICK-a, I'll tell you later."
- "If you play with her," she whispered in my ear, "I won't come over to your house tomorrow."
- So I walked away, feeling a tight knot growing in my belly.
- "I'm having trouble with Katie," I said. "She seems to be really mad at me and I don't know why."
- "You are just *so-o-o-o sensitive* about stuff. Well, I have to do my homework, now."
- "I even think she's been saying bad things about me to my friends so they won't like me," I explained.
- "Katie, does it make you feel good to make me feel bad? Because friends don't do that to friends."
- But now that the secret's out, I don't feel bad anymore.

Intermediate

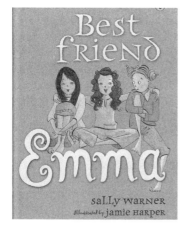

Best Friend Emma by Sally Warner, illustrated by Jamie Harper. New York: Puffin Books, 2007.

> *I am suddenly having a fight with the wrong person. (57)*

Emma McGraw and Annie Pat Masterson are best friends, but Cynthia Harbison has two best friends, Fiona and Heather, and she rank orders them every day. Cynthia is the bossiest girl in Emma's fifth grade class. When Krysten Rodriguez moves to town, Emma wants her to be their friend—not Cynthia's. While Annie Pat is home with the flu, Emma decides to win over Krysten, and then Emma will have two best friends like Cynthia. It's easy to get caught up in the friendship race, but when Annie Pat tells Emma that she is turning into Cynthia, Emma has to stop and think.

This book deals with relational aggression in Cynthia's clique and with Emma's fight to get Krysten away from Cynthia.

Topics for Discussion

1. Cynthia and Emma were friends when Emma first moved to town. What happened to their friendship?
2. What do Emma and Annie Pat have in common?
3. What does Emma want more, to make Kry her friend or to irritate Cynthia?
4. Why is Annie Pat upset with Emma?
5. Cynthia tells Fiona and Heather what to wear to school. Why does she do that? What would happen if Fiona or Heather did not wear what Cynthia tells them to wear?

Quotes for Reader Response

- "Fiona is my first-best friend today, and Heather is my second-best friend," Cynthia is saying. (5)
- And then Cynthia flashes a big kiss-up smile in the new girl's direction. I can already tell that Cynthia is trying to claim Kry for her own. (21)
- "Ms. Sanchez can't make us like each other," Cynthia says, her chin in the air. "Not once we're on the playground. Kids are the boss of that. *I'm* the boss of that, and I decided I don't like you." (32)
- Kry is an equal opportunity smiler. (44)
- "See, Emma's always starting fights," Cynthia pretend-extends to Kry. "But we try to be nice to her, because I guess she can't help it. Her parents are *divorced*," she whispers. (49)
- [Mom] told me that not only did I hurt Annie Pat's feelings, which I did by accident, but I lied about what happened,

which I did on purpose. (But it seemed like a good idea at the time.) (66)

Middle School

Remembering Raquel by Vivian Vande Velde. Orlando: Harcourt, 2007.

> *My first thought, on hearing that Raquel was dead, was: Oh crap. That makes me the class fat girl. (3)*

Overweight Raquel Falcone wasn't popular at Quail Run High School, but after she is struck and killed walking home from a film festival, people stop to reflect on the girl who no one really knew.

Told through many different voices, the story allows us to come to our own conclusions about that last night. There is the police report, including statements from witnesses and the driver; Raquel's blog, which she named Gylindrielle's World; and the thoughts of several people at the funeral home: her father, her best friend Hayley, the staff from school, and other students, including the "popular" girls who shunned her because Raquel was fat.

Many young people envision their own funeral, wonder who would attend, who would be sad, who would feel guilty, who couldn't care less.

Topics for Discussion

1. List the people at the funeral home who genuinely liked Raquel.

2. List those who are there for the show.
3. If Raquel could observe her funeral, how might she react? Would there be any surprises?
4. Why is Raquel different in school than she is at home?
5. Stacy Galbo has some very strange impressions about Raquel. What are they based on? Do these impressions tell us more about Raquel or about Stacy?
6. Through Gylindrielle's World, we get a different view of Raquel. Based only on her blog, what was she like?
7. The circumstances of her death are somewhat confusing. What does the reader know for sure?
8. Raquel was hit by a car, but how did she get in front of that car? Was she pushed, or did she jump, or did she accidentally fall?
9. Sadness is the most common emotion at the funeral, but what other emotions were evident?
10. At some point most of us wonder who would attend our funerals. Why do we do that?

Quotes for Discussion

- Maybe she'd had enough of being nobody's particular friend, of being "that fat girl" in ninth grade. A fast, fatal step to popularity is a possibility to keep in mind. (5)
- I'm just saying . . . someone who can make you laugh might be a better choice for a date than someone who calls you a toad. (21)
- In Gylindrielle's World, all friends are true, and all food is nonfattening. (23)
- And besides not having the looks, she didn't have the clothes, or the voice, or the moves, or most especially: The Attitude. Girls can be merciless. Tough? Girls have got guys beat on that any day. (75)
- Being the most popular girl in the school isn't as easy as you might think. A school takes its whole personality from the attitude set by the "in crowd." And that's quite a responsibility. (81)
- You can be *in* (which is a select few), or you can be *not in* (which is the vast majority), or you can be *out* (but then

you're not out of any crowd, because that's what "out" means). (82)

- When girls grow up in a swarm, they grow up mean. (94)
- You can tell her something you maybe didn't have a chance to say to her, or you can maybe tell her something you liked about her, or something you wish you could say to her, something to celebrate her life. (134)

High School

the beckoners

carrie mac

The Beckoners by Carrie Mac. Victoria, BC: Orca Book Publishers, 2004.

> "That girl is so marked," Simon said as the door slowly shut behind her. "You'd think the air around her would be a different color." (67)

Zoe, her mom, and her little sister Cassy move again for another of her mother's start-overs. In her fifteen years of living, Zoe has moved nine times, and she knows making a connection as a new girl is crucial. This time she makes the wrong connection: Beck is not the warm, friendly, supportive type; she has her own gang—not a clique, but a violent girl gang called the Beckoners—and she wants Zoe to join.

The Beckoners have targeted April since elementary school, but the humiliations have grown into unlawful acts inside and outside of school. For Zoe's initiation, they brand her with a burning fork. After she witnesses the violence that surrounds Beck, she wonders how she got involved. What happened to her moral compass? Who if anyone could stop Beck? And what does Zoe have to endure to get unbranded?

Topics for Discussion

1. Why does Zoe become friends with Beck?
2. Why does she allow herself to be branded? Would anyone allow herself to be branded?
3. Simon seems to be the only one who challenges Beck. Why does she allow that?
4. April's life has been daily torment for years. How has she survived?
5. How does Zoe and April's relationship change throughout the book?
6. What are some of the Beckoners' more violent behaviors?
7. If you were in a class and a gang came in to get someone, what would you do?
8. When did Zoe disappoint you the most? If she didn't ever disappoint you, did anyone in the book? Who?
9. Why isn't the ending realistic?

Quotations for Reader Response

- *At five, she prayed to God that she would wake up one day and be a real dog just like Shadow. At fourteen, she prayed to God she'd never wake up at all.* (2)
- "You've got your skids, your punks, pushers, users, Goths, slags, geeks, hippies, rejects and other standard garden variety misfits . . . the ones that smoke, at least." He sighed. "Home sweet home." (22)
- But you don't walk away from girls like this. You don't turn your back on girls like this unless you're prepared for them to slice you wide open, and not necessarily right away—girls like this were brilliant at simmering resentments. (24)
- Beck had something else in mind, because no matter how hard Zoe tried to avoid her, Beck found her and dragged her along with the Beckoners on their lame movie cliché fieldtrips. (42)
- Still, Dog stared, waiting for Zoe to prove she wasn't like the Beckoners. (44)
- She imagined being there in the damp dark, looking up at this scene. She imagined she was not this person who was about to be branded. (51)

- "You are in so deep. I don't think there's anything left for me to even *say*."
  "But I had to—"
  "I don't see any puppet strings." (57)
- As they pulled away, Zoe turned in her seat and watched another Zoe—Zoe the Beckoner, Zoe the weak, Zoe the bitch—standing at the side of the road, a terribly hurt look on her face, like why was she being left there, all alone in the middle of nowhere with no idea how to get home? Zoe hated her, that's why. (78)
- "What I care about is that everyone treats each other with a little respect. That girl is a brilliant writer, and she's great with kids, and she's sweet and caring and more of a human than either of you two are right now." (107)
- This was just Beck. This wasn't the Beckoners. Just Beck, all by herself. Alone. Beck was just a girl, like her. She wasn't a monster. She had no superpowers. She was mortal like everybody else. (110–11)
- That scar would always be there—a reminder of this mess. (148)

Shattering Glass by Gail Giles. Brookfield, CT: Roaring Brook Press, 2002.

Simon was easy to hate. I never knew exactly why, there was too much to pick from. I guess, really, we each hated him for a different reason, but we didn't realize it until the day we killed him. (1)

Young tells the story of what happened when Rob moves to town. A charismatic leader, he quickly becomes the guy in charge, and his first plan is to turn the class buffoon, Simon Glass, into one of the popular guys. With Young, Coop, and Bob helping, Rob teaches Simon how to dress, dance, and behave in the spotlight. All he has to do is follow every single one of Rob's directions. All are so involved that they miss how the mentally unstable Rob is manipulating them. Simon sees the real Rob and does some manipulating on his own, which earns him Rob's anger. Young, knowing about Rob's secret past, makes special concessions for him, which puts Young in a vulnerable position. Masterfully structured, the story is told after Glass's death, with notes at the beginning of each chapter that provide perspectives from other characters.

Topics for Discussion

1. From the beginning Young does not like Simon. Why?
2. Who is this book about? Rob, Simon, or Young?
3. My computer dictionary defines honor as "strong moral character or strength, and adherence to ethical principles." Using that definition, who is the most honorable person in the book?
4. This is a story of manipulation. Who manipulated? Who was manipulated?
5. Why does Young give up Ronna? Why does Rob ask him to?
6. Explain how each boy's family affected him?
7. Why does Simon sabotage Rob's plan to make him Class Favorite?
8. Explain how Simon and Rob are alike.
9. How does Simon contribute to his own death?
10. Simon loses his life. What did Coop lose? Bob? Rob? Young?
11. Why does Young take the blame when he never swung the bat?

Quotes for Reader Response

- That was so Rob. While his magnetism alone was more than enough to ensure high school deification, he'd still go out of his way to be nice to someone who wasn't even a blip on the useful radar. The nobodies and the somebodies all liked him for it. (6)
- He wasn't happy to have it all; he had to make sure I didn't have anything. (30)

- He snatched the frog and squeezed until the frog's eyes goggled. He placed his index finger against the pad of his thumb and flicked it, striking the frog on its puffed throat. It made a dull, wet smack. "I'll teach you to try and get away." (35)
- But Young did a good thing when he assigned his advance and royalties to Coop. And the best part was that Young did it on his own. This time he knew what was right and he did it. (51)
- I wondered for the hundredth time why this was so necessary to Rob. The only thing I could find was that he needed control the way I needed approval. (100)
- As I wrote, I began to understand more, pulling off layer upon layer of past hints, clues to the inner Rob that I hadn't seen. I knew that no matter what, I'd never betray him. (150)
- The parole board asked how I felt that Rob's been free all these years I've been in prison. I told them. We're all imprisoned in different ways. (173)
- "You're everybody's idea of a 'good' guy, but you're not good because of any convictions or moral compass. You're good because you don't say no. You do as you're told and so far, nobody told you to do anything worng." She pulled her fingers away. "But someday, someone will." (190)
- The expression on Young's face when he looked at me. The bat was still in his hand and there was blood on his cheek. And in his eyes was . . . realization. Knowledge of things nobody that age should have. (203)
- "I don't need a weapon, Rob. All I need to do is say your name. Your real name. Robert Haynes Baddeck, Junior." (211)

ANNOTATED BIBLIOGRAPHY

Some books are appropriate for other levels; I = Intermediate grades, M = middle school, H = high school. Books discussed at length elsewhere in this text are noted parenthetically.

Picture Books

My Secret Bully by Trudy Ludwig, illustrated by Abigail Marble. Ashland, OR: RiverWood Books, 2004. Katie has been Monica's friend since they started school, but lately Katie acts like she doesn't want anyone to see her with Monica; when they are alone, however, she is friendly. Monica decides she needs to tell Katie she doesn't like being treated like that. (See page 81.)

Patty and the Pink Princesses by Terry Slater, illustrated by Sally Springer. New York: Scholastic, 2007. The Pink Princesses won't let Patty join their club because she doesn't have blonde hair and blue eyes. The story ends with the question "How would you feel if you were left out of a group?" Teacher guide is on the back cover.

The Recess Queen by Alexis O'Neill, illustrated by Laura Huliske-Beith. New York: Scholastic, 2002. Mean Jean rules the playground until teeny-tiny Katie Sue shows up. Before she can learn Mean Jean's playground rules, Katie Sue offers friendship.

Yoon and the Jade Bracelet by Helen Recorvits, illustrated by Gabi Swiatkowska. New York: Farrar, Straus and Giroux, 2008. Yoon, a new student from Korea, wants to jump rope with the other girls and hopes to make friends that way, but with a promise of friendship, an older girl tricks Yoon into giving up her jade bracelet.

Intermediate

Amelia's Bully Survival Guide by Marissa Moss. New York: Simon and Schuster, 2006. On the first day of fifth grade, Amelia starts a new notebook. She doesn't know it will be a Bully Survival Guide, but her best friend, Leah, is in another class and Hilary, the meanest girl in class, harasses Amelia from the first day.

Bad Girls by Jacqueline Wilson, illustrated by Nick Sharratt. New York: Delacorte Press, 2001. Ten-year-old Mandy, mommy's little girl with long, blond braids and pink dresses, can't escape the girl bullies at school. Even her former best friend, Melanie, uses their old secrets against her. Then fourteen-year-old Tanya, a wild, punkish foster child, moves in next door and becomes Mandy's trusted friend.

Best Friend Emma by Sally Warner, illustrated by Jamie Harper. New York: Puffin Books, 2007. When her best friend Annie

Pat is home sick, Emma gets caught up in a competition with Cynthia for the new girl's friendship. (See page 82.)

Do Over by Christine Hurley Deriso. New York: Delacorte Press, 2006. In the middle of Elsa's seventh grade year, her mother died suddenly of an aneurysm and then she and her dad move to another town with her grandmother. Elsa has too much to adjust to, but one night her mom makes a special visit to give her a "Do Over" necklace that will help her face a new school and the girl clique led by Darcy. (M)

The Double-Digit Club by Marion Dane Bauer. New York: Holiday House, 2004. The summer after their fourth grade year, best friends Sarah and Paige are the only two girls who have not been invited to join the Double-Digit Club because their tenth birthday falls in the summer. They have vowed not to bend to the pressure, but one does.

Geek Chic: The Zoey Zone by Margie Palatini. New York: HarperCollins, 2008. Accessory-challenged, factoid-spewing Zoey has only 198 days until sixth grade to become chic enough to move away from lunch table ten and join the Bashleys: Brittany and Ashley. A chance encounter with a U GrL photo shoot causes Zoey to appreciate herself and to realize being unique is geek chic. (M)

The Meanest Girl by Debora Allie. New Milford, CT: Roaring Brook Press, 2005. Sixth grade sparkles for Alyssa Fontana until Hayden Martin moves into town and persecutes her; steals her best friend, Chelsea; and makes life generally unbearable. As if that weren't enough, Alyssa also deals with the realization that she is a bully, too. (M)

Nikki & Deja by Karen English, illustrated by Laura Freeman. New York: Clarion Books, 2007. Third graders Nikki and Deja live next door to each other and are best friends until Antonia moves in with her trampoline. After Antonia snubs them, Deja wants to start a club so they can exclude her.

The Quail Club by Carolyn Marsden. Cambridge, MA: Candlewick Press, 2006. For the fifth grade talent show, Thai immigrant Oy hopes to perform a traditional Thai dance, but Liliandra, self-appointed leader of the Quail Club, demands that the club perform an American dance. Oy's mother forbids her to perform Liliandra's offensive dance. No one is willing to stand up to Liliandra, but Oy must find a solution. Sequel to *The Gold Threaded Dress*.

The Skin I'm In by Sharon G. Flake. New York: Jump at the Sun, 2000. Because Maleeka has dark-black skin, the other kids torment her. Miss Saunders, the new English teacher, has a white mark over half her face. Charlese doesn't let up on either of them. (M)

Thank You, Lucky Stars by Beverly Donofrio. New York: Random House, 2008. Best friends Ally Miller and Betsy O'Malley had chosen matching outfits for their first day of fifth grade, but over the summer, Betsy became friends with Mona Montagne and shows up at the bus stop twinned to Mona. New student Tina Tamblin arrives; she is uninhibited, wild, and crazy fun and wears the same tights as Ally. (M)

Middle School

Accidentally Fabulous by Lisa Papademetriou. New York: Scholastic, 2008. Seventh grader Amy Flowers receives a full scholarship to attend the exclusive Allington Academy, and once there she is befriended by Janelle, who is a member of the League—as in They're out of Your League—but Amy slowly realizes how tightly queen bee Fiona Van Steig controls every aspect of the members' lives. The price to join may be too high. (I)

Autobiography of My Dead Brother by Walter Dean Myers, illustrated by Christopher Myers. New York: HarperCollins, 2005. The Counts, a black social club, has been around for over forty years and meets once a month for fellowship. Times have changed and now Rise wants the Counts to support one of their members who robbed a bodega by roughing up the bodega's owner. Rise's new persona pressures the Counts to become a gang. (H)

The Beckoners by Carrie Mac. Victoria, BC: Orca Book Publishers, 2004. Zoe transfers to a new school where Beck and her violent gang seem to rule. Beck decides Zoe must join, but after she is branded with a burning fork, Zoe knows the Beckoners are not for her. (H) (See page 86.)

Cliques, Phonies & Other Baloney by Trevor Romain. Minneapolis: Free Spirit, 1998. With the same format as *Bullies*

Are a Pain in the Brain, this book suggests ways to avoid the cliques and create meaningful, healthy friendships. Nonfiction. (I)

Defying the Diva by D. Anne Love. New York: Simon and Schuster, 2008. Haley, the only ninth grader on the school newspaper, becomes friends with Patrick, the editor. When Camilla Quinn, queen bee/diva, thinks Haley might be interfering with her attempts to snag Patrick, she spreads gossip and manipulates Haley's two best friends into ditching her. Fortunately Haley spends the summer with her aunt in another town where she rebuilds her self-confidence while working at a resort. (I)

The Devil's Toenail by Sally Prue. New York: Scholastic, 2004. Thirteen-year-old Steve Saunders starts a new school after being bullied at his old one and joins a group of boys with Daniel as their bully/leader to find protection, but soon Steve lives in fear. (I)

Drowning Anna by Sue Mayfield. New York: Hyperion Books, 2002. Thirteen-year-old Anna Goldsmith moves to a town and a new school where Hayley chooses Anna to be her new best friend, and then Hayley drops Anna. Told in flashbacks after Anna has tried to kill herself, this book weaves together Anna's journal, her mother's bedside hospital watch, and the reflections of her friend, Melanie. (H)

Freak by Marcella Pixley. New York: Farrar, Straus and Giroux, 2007. Though everyone tries to fancy her up, Miriam doesn't want to make the transition to middle school like the other girls did, and for that she earns the nickname Freak. (H)

Gilda Joyce: The Ladies of the Lake by Jennifer Allison. New York: Dutton Children's Books, 2006. Thirteen-year-old Gilda Joyce earns a scholarship to Our Lady of Sorrows, a private girls school, where she tries to solve the mystery of a girl's death. (I)

The Girls by Amy Goldman Koss. New York: Dial Books, 2000. Middle school cliques can be very cruel, and Koss shows one from the inside. Powerful Candace decides who is in and who is rejected according to her whims. Told in the voices of five members of the group in the beginning of the book, we see what happens when Candace tires of Maya. (I)

Itch by Michelle D. Kwasney. New York: Henry Holt, 2008. Twelve-year-old Delores Colchester, called Itch, and her gram are forced to move from Florida to a trailer park in Ohio after the death of her gramps. Trying to fit in with the Breck Girls forces Itch to discover more about herself.

Jumped by Rita Williams Garcia. New York: Amistad, 2009. Leticia loves to share the latest gossip. Dominique wants either Mr. Hershheiser to change her grade or the coach to change her eligibility rule so she can play basketball. New girl Trina knows she's cute, artsy, and bubbly and believes everyone envies her. The story is told in the voices of these three sophomore girls on the day Leticia overhears Dominique threaten to beat up Trina after school. (H)

Kiss Me Kill Me by Lauren Henderson. New York: Delacorte Press, 2008. Scarlett Wakefield is sixteen and in a posh private school outside London where Plum Saybourne, queen bee of the Smart Set, invites Scarlett to one of her elite parties. Alone on the garden terrace, Scarlett and Dan McAndrew are kissing when he has an allergic reaction and dies in Scarlett's arms. After an inconclusive inquest, Scarlett transfers to Wakefield Hall Collegiate but stays determined to solve the mystery of Dan's death. (H)

The Losers' Club by John Lekich. Toronto: Annick Press, 2002. Jerry Whitman and the other "haves" make life miserable for the "have-nots" at Marshall McLuhan High School. Alex Sherwood, dubbed Savior by the Losers' Club, has cerebral palsy and walks with crutches.

Mars 1 by Fuyumi Soryo. Los Angeles: Tokyopop, 2002. Rei likes to ride on the edge, and could have his pick of any of the top girls, but Kira, a quiet artist, makes quite an impression on him. Kira is sexually assaulted by one of the teachers and bullied by the girls before Rei protects her. Graphic novel.

Peer Pressure: Deal with It without Losing Your Cool by Elaine Slavens, illustrated by Ben Shannon. Toronto: James Lorimer, 2004. Part of the Deal with It series, this workbook talks about peer pressure and the Insider, the Outsider, and the Witness, with spot quizzes to be sure everyone understands. Presented with colorful graphics. (I)

The Plain Janes by Cecil Castellucci and Jim Rugg. New York: MINX/DC Comics, 2007. After experiencing a terrorist attack in Metro City, Jane and her family move away from the city to attend Buzz Aldrin High School. Wisely avoiding the "cool girls," she decides to sit at a lunch table with three loners, Jayne, Jane, and Polly Jane, who she unites in an underground art lovers group.

Poison Ivy by Amy Goldman Koss. New York: Roaring Brook Press, 2006. Ms. Gold has her government classes conduct a mock trial on an issue present in their school. She convinces Ivy to bring charges against her three alleged tormentors, Ann, Sophie, and Benita. Everyone in the school has watched these three harass Ivy since early elementary when they started calling her Poison Ivy. The jury of students brings in what they believe is their only safe verdict. (See chapter 2, page 15.)

Pretty Tough by Liz Tigelaar. New York: Razorbill, 2007. Charlie Brown, sophomore, has been an outcast since her best friend, Regan Holder, turned on her last year and spread rumors that Charlie was a lesbian. Charlie's sister Krista, older by two years, is one of the beautiful, popular girls, and she can't understand why Charlie can't be more like her. (H)

Queen Bee by Chynna Clugston. New York: Scholastic, 2005. In this graphic novel, Haley Madison has spent time preparing for her new school so she will not be a geek again. Though Haley is in solid with the "top clique," Alexa Harmon arrives and a war begins.

Queen of the Toilet Bowl by Frieda Wishinsky. Victoria, BC: Orca Soundings, 2005. Renata and her family left Brazil after her father died. Now in the United States, Renata works hard to be invisible in her elite school so nobody will discover her mother supports them by cleaning houses. But queen bee Liz finds out and floods the Internet with photos of Renata's mother with her head in a toilet bowl. The school deals with the situation immediately, and there is much verbal support for Renata's courage and horror about the "Internet bullying." (I)

Remembering Raquel by Vivian Vande Velde. Orlando: Harcourt, 2007. Raquel was never part of the popular girls' clique because she was overweight, but at her funeral, everyone wants the attention of being her best friend. (See page 84.)

Responsible by Darlene Ryan. Victoria, BC: Orca Book Publishers, 2007. Kevin Frasier and Erin Tennant each choose a different way to deal with the vicious bully Nick, but all paths intersect in this realistic portrayal of the costs—and benefits—of doing the right thing.

Returnable Girl by Pamela Lowell. Tarrytown, NY: Marshall Cavendish, 2006. Thirteen-year-old Ronnie's lying and stealing has landed her in her very last chance foster home with Alison, a counselor. At her new school, Ronnie maneuvers her way into Paige's circle of friends, but her friendship with outcast Cat might get her ejected from the in crowd.

The Smell of Old Lady Perfume by Claudia Guadalupe Martinez. El Paso: Cinco Punto Press, 2008. The night before Chela Gonzalez starts sixth grade, her father has a stroke, and everything in her life changes. When he comes home from the hospital a week later, Chela returns to school. There Chela discovers that her best friend, Nora, is now part of Camila's group, and Camila does not like Chela. (I)

Something to Blog About by Shana Norris. New York: Amulet Books, 2008. Angel has bullied Libby since kindergarten, and now in tenth grade it only gets worse when Libby's mom and Angel's dad start dating. At a peace dinner, Angel slips into Libby's bedroom and sends her Internet journal out to everyone at school.

Tribes by Arthur Slade. New York: Random House, 2002. After the disappearance of his father, Percy escapes into the safe analytical world of science as he studies the different tribes in his high school: the Jock Tribe, the Born-Again Tribe, the Grunge Tribe, and others. (H)

High School

Boys over Flowers: Hana Yori Dango, vol. 1, by Yoko Kamio. San Francisco: VIZ Media, 2003. F4, the most elite boy at Eitoku Academy, creates the school's social rules and the elite girls do anything to attract his attention, but harassing Tsukushi seems to be this year's fun project. Graphic novel. (M)

The Brothers Torres by Coert Voorhees. New York: Hyperion Books, 2008. Frankie has always looked up to his older brother Steve, but now Steve seems on a path contrary to all their family's values in joining the Cholos. When Frankie finds his path, he runs straight into his brother.

The Dream Where Losers Go by Beth Goobie. Victoria, BC: Orca Book Publishers, 2006. Skey is in a lock-down unit after trying to commit suicide. When she is allowed to return to school, Jigger, her boyfriend and head of their gang, the Dragons, reenters her life. Slowly the memory of why she tried to kill herself resurfaces: she was gang raped at Jigger's instruction.

Edge by Diane Tullson, Toronto: Stoddart Kids, 2002. After joining a group of misfits, ninth grader Marlie Peters has to decide if belonging to a group is worth giving up what she believes is right.

Evolution, Me & Other Freaks of Nature by Robin Brande. New York: Alfred A. Knopf, 2007. Mena Reese enters ninth grade ostracized by all her former Christian friends because she could not support their harassment of a perceived-to-be-gay student, Danny Pierce, who moved away. This year's conflict is the evolution versus intelligent design debate, and the complications keep multiplying. (M)

Kiss & Blog by Alyson Noël. New York: St. Martin's Griffin, 2007. Winter and Sloan practice all summer to create perfect images for tenth grade, but when Sloan sees her chance to be the next Pink Princess, she not only ditches Winter, she turns the other sophomore girls against her. Winter starts an on-line blog where she journals her feelings, and though she never uses any names, everyone knows somebody who fits the Sloan role. (M)

New Blood by Peter McPhee. Toronto: James Lorimer, 2007. After being viciously beaten by three older teens, fourteen-year-old Callum and his parents move from Scotland to Winnipeg where Callum's older brother Ewan and his wife live. But on the first day, Callum's accent draws the attention of Rick and his gang of thugs, and someone has filmed Rick throwing Callum through the air and posted it on a blog site for the whole school to see. (M)

Ouran High School: Host Club by Bisco Hatori. San Francisco: VIZ Media, 2005. The Host Club of Ouran High School has only the wealthiest, most handsome males as members, and when Haruhi, a scholarship student, accidentally breaks a very expensive vase at a club party, the members decide she must work off the damages. Graphic novel.

Played by Dana Davidson. New York: Hyperion Books, 2005. Ian Striver, a handsome junior in a large Detroit high school, pledges an underground fraternal group, Freaky Boys Incorporated (FBI). His initiation dictates he must date, seduce, and prove it to the other FBIs—in three weeks. Kylie, the plain girl selected at random, has much to learn—and much to teach—as the story unravels.

Quad by C. G. Watson. New York: Razorbill, 2007. Told in multiple perspectives of the school's groups—Freaks, Choirboys, Drama Queens, Jock/Steroid Posses, Preps, and Techies—and in different time settings, the past with all its adolescent posing and bullying and the present where there has just been a shooting on campus, six students hide in a locked storage room and listen for clues of what is happening outside.

The Queen of Cool by Cecil Castellucci. Cambridge, MA: Candlewick Press, 2007. Libby sees herself as the Queen of Cool and her in-crowd supports that idea, but when she gets an internship at the Los Angeles Zoo and teams with losers Shelton and Tina, Libby starts to think more clearly. (M)

The Secret Rites of Social Butterflies by Lizabeth Zindel. New York: Viking, 2008. At Berkeley Prep, Maggie attracts the attention of the Revelers, a social group led by Victoria, and after her pledge week, they tell her about The Wall—where they record secrets of the school. The secrets give the Revelers "leverage" over certain others, from students to teachers, and now even over Maggie.

See No Evil by Diane Young. Victoria, BC: Orca Currents, 2006. On their way home from school, Shawn and Daniel take the shortcut behind the mall, but on this trip they see three guys beating up someone. Then the one giving the orders sees them. Daniel shouts, "Run." The next day they decide not to tell the police, but when Shawn sees two of the guys pulling Daniel behind the mall, he runs to get the security guards. (M)

Sewer Rats by Sigmund Brouwer. Victoria, BC: Orca Currents, 2006. Jim McClosky, Lisa Chambers, Micky Downs, and the Cooper twins, Al and Dave, make up the Sewer Rats with Carter Saylor ready to join. After his initiation, the Sewer

Rats take the challenge of a group from Medford to a paint war in the city's sewers. (M)

Shattering Glass by Gail Giles. Brookfield, CT: Roaring Book Press, 2002. Rob is the charismatic kid who moves to town and becomes the new leader for the males. He manipulates losers into the top clique and former winners into loser status. From the opening page, the reader knows who will die and wonders why they all go along with Rob's plan. (See page 88.)

Swimming with the Sharks by Debbie Reed Fischer. Woodbury, MN: Flux, 2008. Even though she is a junior, Peyton Grady has made the senior cheerleading squad at a posh private school. Captain Lexie Court takes cheerleading very seriously, so when Ellika Garrett, short, round, and unattractive, buys her way onto the squad, Lexie organizes the others to torment her till she quits. When their tactics go beyond hazing, "Smellika" ends up in the hospital.

Walking Naked by Alyssa Brugman. New York: Delacorte Press, 2004. Megan Twu is not only part of the eleventh grade in group, she leads it. If someone strays, she calls for an intervention. But when she gets put in detention with Perdita Wiguiggan, the school freak, Megan starts to befriend Perdita, against every rule of her group.

NOTE

1. Trevor Romain, *Cliques, Phonies & Other Baloney* (Minneapolis: Free Spirit, 1998), 12–18.

6

The "Isms": Prejudice Based on Race, Culture, Religion, Gender, or Other Differences

Human beings come in many varieties. While some of us delight in these differences, some of us are suspicious, and some even feel threatened. Others believe they have the right, indeed the responsibility, to change those who are different and step into another's personal space. I don't know where hate comes from, but I have seen it show up in various degrees of intensity and target a wide range of differences. It can destroy a classroom, a school, a community—to say nothing of human lives.

In *A Perfect Snow* by Nora Martin, a small town in Montana has attracted a new minister and his followers. They call themselves the Guardians of Identity; I would call them white racists. A depressed and unemployed father gets drawn into the congregation and pulls in his two sons. *Yellow Line*, a Romeo-and-Juliet type of story by Sylvia Olsen, tells the story of a suburb in western Canada, split between the whites and the Indians, or First Nation, that has to accept a white girl and a First Nation boy who have fallen in love. A picture book, *My Name Is Bilal* by Asma Mobin-Uddin, brings us the problems of Bilal and his sister Ayesha, who are Muslim, on their first day of school. Most of the picture books I have included deal with animals learning to accept differences. Others like *Let's Talk about Race* by Julius Lester and *Grandpa, Is Everything Black Bad?* by Sandy Lynne Holman help to educate children about prejudices before they form.

I am a pretty easy-going, do-no-harm type of person. I believe most people do the best they can with what they have experienced, but I also believe we can grow out of prejudices. I have tried to present some books that may protect the young people in your classes and libraries. What I believe in most is everyone's right to be safe. As a teacher I believe creating a safe space is my first responsibility to my students. In my classroom and in my presence, I want each of them to feel safe enough to learn. An individual who is afraid cannot learn to his or her ability level.

My mission for this chapter is to provide books that will educate people about some of the diversities in our society. My hope is that in reading these books, more children will be safe in your classroom, in your library, in your school and neighborhood, and always in your presence.

FOCUS BOOKS

Picture Book

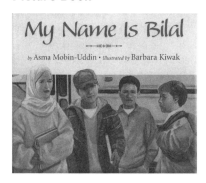

My Name Is Bilal by Asma Mobin-Uddin, illustrated by Barbara Kiwak. Honesdale, PA: Boyds Mills Press, 2005.

> *Bilal tried to pay attention, but all he could think about was Scott's mean stare and the way Scott had laughed at his sister.*

On his first day in the new school, Bilal watches from a distance as two boys harass his sister, Ayesha, about her headscarf, but he does nothing. Later in class he says his name is Bill. The teacher, Mr. Ali, who is also Muslim, looks confused. That night at evening prayers, Mr. Ali gives Bilal a book, *Bilal Ibn Radah, Friend and Helper of the Prophet*, who "was the first person to give the Muslim call to prayer during the time of Prophet Muhammad, peace be upon him." As Bilal reads the book, he learns how the earlier Bilal had suffered for his belief, and the boy gains courage from the story.

The next day when the same two boys start to bully his sister, Bilal goes to her side and tells the boys to leave his sister alone. When the two boys leave, Bilal apologizes for not standing up for her the day before. After school he plays basketball with some boys at the park. One boy has to leave early. Bilal discovers that boy is also Muslim and he is going to pray. Bilal catches up with the other boy and suggests they pray together.

Topics for Discussion

1. In all religions, there are traditional practices. What are two of the traditions in the Muslim faith that are mentioned in the book?
2. When the boys pull at Ayesha's headscarf, what does that tell you about them?
3. Has anyone ever teased you about your beliefs?
4. Why is it important to learn about other people's beliefs?

Quotes for Reader Response

- Bilal wishes his family had never left Chicago. At his old school, there had been lots of Muslim kids. Here, it seemed there were none.
- "Son, why did you say your name was Bill?"
  "Because I want to be like everybody else. Nobody else in the class has a name like Bilal."
- "If this is America, I can wear what I want," Ayesha said, lifting her head defiantly. "And I want to cover my hair. Now please move."
- "My sister and I are Muslims. . . . And America *is* our country. We were born here."

Intermediate

Feathers by Jacqueline Woodson. New York: G. P. Putnam's Sons, 2007.

> *"I guess that's how hope is too—all light and everything like that [feathers]. There's hope in this house. And at your church. . . . At our school. Across the highway and on this side too. Everywhere." (80)*

In 1971, Frannie and her family live on one side of the highway and white people live on the other side. Then one day a seemingly

white boy enrolls in Frannie's sixth grade class—and no one can stop staring at him. At home, Frannie's brother, Sean, is deaf: he lives with another type of discrimination. At the Rec Center or at school, some kids, particularly the pretty girls that Sean wants so much to meet, just stare at him and say it's a shame. In both places few people take the time to communicate.

Frannie's class has just studied an Emily Dickinson poem with the line "Hope is the thing with feathers." Frannie believes she finally understands; hope, like feathers, floats everywhere, on both sides of the highway, in their school, and in her home.

Topics for Discussion

1. When does this book take place? What was happening in the United States at that time?
2. There are two types of prejudice in this book. What are they?
3. How are Trevor and the Jesus Boy alike? Different?
4. Describe Rayray at the beginning of the book and then at the end of the book.
5. "Hope is the thing with feathers." Give examples of hope in this book.
6. Ms. Johnson gives an assignment to write all the ways the people in her class are alike. Why is that such a good assignment?
7. Make a list of how you and the people in your class are alike.
8. Identify the people in this book who feel different from everyone else. Explain why they might feel that way.

9. Life has changed since 1971. Compare the book to the present day. What has changed? What hasn't changed?
10. At the end of the book, how has Trevor changed?

Quotes for Reader Response

- *"Welcome to the seventies, Frannie. Sounds like Ms. Johnson's trying to tell you all something about looking forward instead of back all the time."* (3)
- "Don't no palefaces go to this school. You need to get your white butt back across the highway." (4)
- Seems kids on this side of the highway were always trying to figure out ways to fly and run and cross over things and . . . get free or something. (21)
- "Nah," I head Rayray say softly. "You heard the brother-man. He's just like a little bit lost. It be's like that sometimes." (27)
- I don't know if I believe in miracles. I think things happen and we need to believe in them. (31)
- "People always wonder about the new kid—you know that. You were the new kid once." (46)
- "I ain't your man, white boy!" The Jesus Boy looked at him calmly and said, "Well, I ain't your white boy, man." (66)
- *"Because you already have both worlds, Frannie. You can walk wherever you want."* (83)
- "My mama isn't white and my daddy isn't white and as far as I know it, you're the one with the white daddy living across the highway." (88)
- "I ain't scared of Trevor anymore," Rayray said. "I'm not going to let him hit me in the head anymore either. I bet none of us gonna be scared of him. He's just like us. Just a kid. You don't need to be scared of no kid." (91)
- "Now, what we're going to do this morning," she said, her voice becoming all bright again, "is write down all the things we all have in common." (105)`

Middle School

Rebound by Bob Krech. Tarrytown, NY: Marshall Cavendish, 2006.

So maybe it's not just about black and white. (225)

Usually the Polish guys go out for wrestling and the black guys go out for basketball, but Ray Wisniewski and Stan Prusakowski love basketball, and their senior year, they both make the team. However, old prejudices die slowly and new prejudices seem to come out of nowhere. Ray's oldest friend, Walter, isn't as open to friendship with blacks as Ray and Pruze; some of the black players are not accepting of the two new white players; and others simply respect a guy for who he is. People change, and sometimes friendships have to end; but it doesn't always have to be about race.

Topics for Discussion

1. Is Ray prejudiced in the beginning of the book? What were some of things that show he might have been?
2. There are several scenes in the book that show Walter as a kind, thoughtful person. List some of them and explain how that fits with his racism.
3. Ray's Polish neighborhood is really quite small. What are some examples of how the families are interconnected?
4. How do Ray and Walter each change during the book?
5. How do these changes affect their friendship?
6. The guys on the team tease each other with words that are linked to their races. Discuss how that is or is not racism.
7. Who is more racist, Walter or Rudy? Support your answer.
8. What can you do if your good friend behaves in a way that you believe is prejudiced or unjust?

9. How can a person become comfortable with people of other races?
10. If Coach T asked you, how would you define yourself?
11. How are a person's values linked to his race?
12. What helps a person form his values?

Quotes for Reader Response

- After a couple of games, the rest of the guys start acting real regular with me. Talking and joking and stuff. Especially Al and Tyrone. It's a whole new thing. I was never ever talking to black guys like this before. (67)
- Tyrone spits at him [Robert], "You listen to me, Little Black Fauntleroy! You better play serious, tight D right now!" (72)
- On our whole squad of twenty-six ballplayers, there's only three of us who are white. Meanwhile there are twelve cheerleaders and two are black. Figure that one out. (115)
- "Look. I know you're into the b-ball thing and you gotta play with these savages. But who says you have to dance with them and hang out with them?" (125)
- I can't deal with Robert being my personal coach. "Coach, I don't know if this would actually work out real well." He doesn't even blink. "Raymond. You will *make* it work." (156)
- Black lips had been on the cup. I embarrassed myself again. That I even thought about it. I take a nice long drink and pass it back. (173)
- Pruze stands there. He is not smiling. "I'm serious, Ray. Watch yourself with him [Walter]." (179)
- This is not all fitting together. "I thought you were president of the Multicultural Club." Her eyes flash angrily. "That's school. That's not double-dating in public, Ray." (217)
- "Five Spades! Whoop! Whoop! Five Spades! Whoop! Whoop!" (230)
- "White is right! We're gonna fight! White is right! We're gonna fight!" (231)
- "You're going to have to decide who is going to define you." No one says anything. "It is my hope you will have the courage to define yourselves." (234)

- So, Robert finally had to move off of Rudy to do the right thing. And I had to move off of Walter to do the same. A brotherhood of actions. Of deeds. (269)

Yellow Line by Sylvia Olsen. Victoria, BC: Orca Book Publishers, 2005.

> I want the whole world to shut up. I want every-thing to slow down so I can figure out what the hell is happening to me. (29)

Vince and Sherry have been best friends since birth, but he really doesn't understand her lately. Their village has always been separated from the next village, where the Indians, or First Nation, live. All the kids go to the same school in the city, but an imaginary yellow line divides everywhere else, even the school bus. The Indians sit in the front of the bus and the whites sit in the back. Sherry has started sitting as close to the front as she can, and Steve is sitting as far back as he can, and they talk all the way to school! Vince gets a tight feeling, because he doesn't remember anyone crossing the line before or the rule, "Stick to your own kind."

This contemporary retelling of Romeo and Juliet revisits the conflict between the older generation's prejudices and the younger generation's need to cross those old lines.

Topics for Discussion

1. How can an imaginary line be so powerful?
2. Why does everyone accept the complete separation of these two communities?

3. What are Vince's beliefs about integration at the beginning of the book?
4. How do Vince's beliefs compare to those of his parents?
5. The young people from the two small villages go to school in the city with other young people from different areas. How does that influence their views on segregation and integration?
6. At the city school, Steve is one of the most popular students. The author doesn't tell us if dating Sherry is a problem at school. What do you think?
7. How is the bus an important setting?
8. Does it surprise you to know this book is set on the west coast of Canada?
9. Vince and Sherry's parents would not call themselves prejudiced, but they are; and, they want their children to have the same beliefs. Do many young people just take their parents beliefs for their own? How difficult is it to choose other beliefs?

Quotations for Reader Response

- We all lived by the rule of the yellow line. (5)
- The rules of separation in our village are clear and everyone knows them. The most important rule is: Date your own kind. (11)
- Sherry's acting like Steve's her boyfriend. The worst part of it is she looks like she doesn't think there's anything wrong with it. (26)
- At the next stop, Steve gets on and walks straight down the aisle as if he's done it every day of his life and plunks himself next to Sherry. In one move, he blows away years of school bus seating arrangements. (35)
- "If she wants to hang out with Steve, that's up to her." (58)
- "What's crap is all that stuff about sticking to your own, and Indians being drunk and stoned and no good for us. Steve's the best thing in my life. . . . He's the one who tells me to do my homework and respect my parents." (63–64)
- "Let me tell you something, son. If you're sorry for something then pick up the bat, step up to the plate and play

the ball. It ain't going to do you no good walking down a dark road in the rain talking to yourself for the rest of your life." (87)

- "Mr. Porter," Steve says. He steps closer and looks Donnie in the eye. "I'm sorry for any trouble I have caused your family, but Sherry and I like each other. I don't want our relationship to get in the way of her family or her education. But I don't want to stop seeing her either." (91)
- It's like my feet are standing on the ground for the first time in my life. It's like, I'm Vince Hardy and I don't have to be afraid or embarrassed or apologetic. (106)

High School

The Confessional by J. L. Powers. New York: Alfred A. Knopf, 2007.

"Sometimes I get the feeling I'm marching blindly toward something I don't want to be." *(97)*

In El Paso's Jesuit High School, the all-male student population is diverse, made up of U.S. citizens, Mexican citizens, and Mexicans living in the United States. Though some teasing and typical harassment goes on, most of the student body seems to get along fairly well.

After a war of words where Bernie Martinez shouted homophobic slurs at MacKenzie Malone, a fight breaks out between the two. Bernie pushes Mac until something clicks in Mac's head, and he just keeps kicking Bernie even after he is down. Father Raymond pulls Mac off, but a battered Bernie is rushed to the hospital. Mac gets suspended for three weeks. Later that night, Mac is attacked in his front yard and stabbed several times, later dying at the hospital. There aren't any witnesses.

The rest of the book is told through several flashbacks and six different voices: MacKenzie Malone, Isaiah Contreras, Greg Gonzalez, Daniel Tucker, Alex Gold, and Jim Hill. The book is a puzzle, not only in the mystery of who committed the murder, but also in the multiple story pieces that slowly fit together. In the beginning the students of Jesuit High School seem to be friendly in their racial and homophobic banter. Prejudice does not cause the murder, but it is the cause or excuse for the violence that follows. Readers need to be observant and read for detail.

Topics for Discussion

1. It the beginning of the story, do most students at Jesuit High School believe there is little prejudice there?
2. Bernie and Mac are the two involved in the initial fight. Was their fight based in prejudice?
3. Was Mac's murder a racist hate crime? What evidence suggests it was?
4. Who or what fuels the hidden prejudices that cause the students to get violent?
5. How many types of prejudice are there in this book?
6. What racial, cultural, or other epithets are used during the course of the story?
7. Jim Hill is a bit crazy, but he is very good at manipulating people. Cite some examples.
8. Alex Gold does not have any friends. What does his invisibility enable him to do?
9. How is Isaiah different from the other kids? What helped mold him into a pacifist?

Quotations for Reader Response

- Peaceful resistance . . . what a concept. (15)
- It's weird to think about how other people see you when you can't see yourself. (33)
- See, in my family, it works like this: Dad gets a little violent with Mom and we try to pretend like it was nothing—it's not nothing. (43)
- There is an upside to being invisible: I see *a lot*. (72)
- If I can find the most likely suspect, I can fan the flames. Imagine the whole school going up in smoke. That would be sweet. (152)

- Idiots come in all shades. (184)
- Nothing's been the same since The Fight on Friday, and everything's changed even more drastically in these last few minutes. Nobody knows who anybody else is. But we all know there are enemies among us. Maybe even a killer. (201)
- Pacifism, whatever it is, is a tough road to take. I've seen the destruction violence causes. (206)
- The level of ignorance scares me. (239)
- "My mom says that if you get mad and act on it, you could do something you'll regret, something you can't ever fix." (251)
- "You have to stand up for things." (254)

A Perfect Snow by Nora Martin. New York: Bloomsbury, 2002.

> *I hated the fact that anger had taken over my brain, if it even was anger. Maybe it was just habit. (75–76)*

Seventeen-year-old Ben Campbell, his younger brother David, and his parents are new to Logette, Montana, and trying to make a new start. Mr. Campbell, a former ranch manager, hasn't been able to find a job, but he has found a church that speaks to him—Guardians of the Identity. Lonn, the preacher, believes in superior white identity and preaches what Mr. Campbell wants to hear—others are to blame for most of the problems in the world. Ben and David attend with their dad who pushes them to get involved. One night Ben does. Chuck and Travis, part of Lonn's inner circle, suggest Ben join them on that night's assignment. Outside a Jewish business, they spray paint cultural epithets and torch the car sitting in front of the building, allowing Ben the honor of throwing the flaming match onto the gasoline-soaked vehicle. Later events include shooting out the windows and defacing a "Jew church" and terrorizing the home of Trenton Biggs, a perceived-to-be-gay student at Ben's school.

Soon, Ben's brother David joins them and gets hooked on the excitement at the same time Ben's conscience catches up with him. While Ben does community service, David does community dis-service. Before long the danger of the events escalates.

People who join hate groups usually do so out of frustration, fear, and anger, a dangerous combination. They are looking for someone who supports their frustration. The Southern Poverty Law Center maintains an excellent website covering many issues, hate groups being one of them. At www.splcenter.org you will find a hate group map that will provide the number of hate groups in each state in the United States of America. Click on your state to see where hate groups are located and their "hate speciality." Pennsylvania has an archived website, the Network Website of the Pennsylvania Alliance for Democracy, or PAD-NET (www.padnet.org). Though the website is no longer active, the link "Civil Rights and Non-Violence Guidelines" provides information on what to do if a hate group starts in your town. It also links to the Southern Poverty Law Center.

Topics for Discussion

1. How would you define the term "hate group"?
2. Using that definition, is Guardians of the Identity a hate group? Explain.
3. Mr. Campbell has always been a responsible father and provider for his family. How have unemployment and Lonn's church changed him?
4. What seem to be the beliefs of the Guardians of the Identity? How does Lonn promote these?
5. Ben develops an unlikely friendship with Jason. How do they help each other?
6. What is Eden's role in the book?
7. Ben participates in three of Lonn's nighttime raids. The first raid energizes and excites him. Why? How did the third raid affect him?

8. When Ben and David's mother knew the truth, she did not hesitate in calling the police. Why did she act so quickly?
9. Compare how Ben, David, and Jason each change through the course of the book.
10. Ben narrates the story. How do you think the story would have changed if David had told it from his point of view?
11. Religion is supposed to be a positive thing in people's lives. How, then, do negative actions sometimes come from religious organizations?

Quotes for Reader Response

- "A RETCH," I told him, "is a kid who's rich enough to cheat." (7)
- "God didn't intend for the races to mix, making everyone into mud people," Lonn said. "And since that boy's mother is from Nam, he is impure." (16)
- I didn't know if I understood everything Lonn said, but I felt myself being drawn toward him. (18)
- Making that car burn almost made up for every dirty look, every name hissed at me from under some creep's breath. (23–24)
- "We whites are God's true children! We will no longer tolerate the pollution of our place by Jews and their colored followers." (58)
- "These guys aren't the warriors you think they are. They're just criminals hiding behind a cause." (84)
- I had taught my brother a lot, including how to be a bully. (106)
- Mom shook her head, "Our life from the very beginning has been wrong. It must have been. . . . Our life taught you to hate people you didn't even know. Our life taught you to blame other people for your problems. I am responsible for that life." (126)
- "I'm not only trailer trash but a criminal as well. So how do I get out?"
  "Start over?" Jason suggested. (133)

ANNOTATED BIBLIOGRAPHY

Some books are appropriate for other levels; I = intermediate grades, M = middle school, H = high school. Books discussed at length elsewhere in this text are noted parenthetically.

Picture Books

All Families Are Special by Norma Simon, illustrated by Teresa Flavin. Morton Grove, IL: Albert Whitman, 2003. After Mrs. Mack announces she will soon be a grandmother, she and her students talk about their families and they realize there are many different types of families.

All Kinds of Children by Norma Simon, illustrated by Diane Paterson. Morton Grove, IL: Albert Whitman, 1999. Children all over the world have things in common, from having belly buttons to wearing clothes to holding on to special things. Children are more alike than different.

Children of Asian America compiled by the Asian American Coalition, photographs by Gene H. Mayeda. Chicago: Polychrome, 1995. Each of these thirteen stories contains an American child with a different Asian heritage representing thirteen different Asian countries. Some of these children face two bullies—the American child and the other Asian children; some have bullies in their history—like the Japanese whose families came to the United States in the early 1900s. (I/M/H)

Do unto Otters—A Book about Manners by Laurie Keller. New York: Henry Holt, 2007. Mr. Rabbit gets worried when the new neighbors are Otters. He doesn't know any otters and he has never met an otter—they are different! Then Owl tells him to "treat otters the same way you'd like otters to treat you."

The Family Book by Todd Parr. New York: Little, Brown, 2003. Using human and animal families displayed through colorful graphics, Parr writes about ways families are different and alike.

Four Hens and a Rooster by Lena Landström, translated by Joan Sandin, illustrated by Olof Landström. Stockholm, Sweden:

Raben and Sjogren Books, 2005. Four hens live in a chicken yard with one rooster, who is always too busy to talk to them. One day the hens notice that their part of the feed trough is much smaller than the rooster's. When they approach the rooster with their thoughts, he crows, "Hens shouldn't think!" He yelled so loudly one hen fainted. After several other such scenes, the hens decide to take a self-esteem class. They return and divide the feed trough into five equal parts.

Grandpa, Is Everything Black Bad? by Sandy Lynne Holman, illustrated by Lela Kometiani. Davis, CA: Culture Coop, 1995. A little boy recounts to his grandpa the many ways black usually means something bad. Grandpa then explains the proud African Montsho heritage that goes with their dark skin.

It's Okay to Be Different by Todd Parr. New York: Little, Brown, 2001. Using human and animal families displayed through colorful graphics, Parr shows ways that being different is okay.

Jungle Drums by Graeme Base. New York: Harry N. Abrams, 2004. Everyone knows warthogs get the least respect because they are not as cool as the other animals, until Ngiri, the smallest warthog in all of Africa, plays the magic drums.

Let's Talk about Race by Julius Lester, illustrated by Karen Barbour. New York: Amistad, 2005. Told in first person, Julius Lester talks about race and asks simple questions that lead readers to the understanding that we are all so much more than our skin.

Mr. Lincoln's Way by Patricia Polacco. New York: Philomel Books, 2001. Though Mr. Lincoln's skin is dark, he is an everything kind of guy and the best principal in the whole world. Ask anyone in his school, except for Eugene "Mean Gene" Esterhause. Mean Gene bullies everyone, but Mr. Lincoln sees something more in Eugene besides the cruel words he has learned at home.

My Name Is Bilal by Asma Mobin-Uddin, illustrated by Barbara Kiwak. Honesdale, PA: Boyds Mills Press, 2005. Bilal and his sister Ayesha move to a new school, where they are harassed because they are Muslim. (See page 102.)

The Playground Problem by Margaret McNamara, illustrated by Mike Gordon. New York: Aladdin Paperbacks, 2004. During first grade recess, the boys play soccer, but when Emma asks

if she can play, the boys all agree that girls cannot play soccer. Emma is furious, but that night her dad helps her come
up with a plan. The next day, Emma and the girls play soccer
on their own, and soon the boys realize girls and boys can
play on the same team.

Intermediate

Defending Irene by Kristin Wolden Nitz. Atlanta: Peachtree,
2004. Irene, thirteen, and her family move to the Italian Alps
for a year. No one expects the new kid from America to speak
Italian, and no one believes she wants to play soccer on the
boys' team, since girls shouldn't do things like that. (M)

Feathers by Jacqueline Woodson. New York: G. P. Putnam's
Sons, 2007. Set in 1971, Frannie and her family live on one
side of the highway and the white people live on the other
side, but she and her friends have a new experience when a
new student shows up and he looks white. (See page 103.)

A Friendship for Today by Patricia C. McKissack. New York:
Scholastic, 2007. Set in Missouri in 1954, after the Supreme
Court has just ruled all schools must be integrated, twelve-
year-old Rosemary starts her sixth grade year in a formerly
all-white school. (M)

Getting in the Game by Dawn FitzGerald. New Milford, CT:
Roaring Brook Press, 2005. Feisty seventh grader Joanna
Giordano fights to get on the boys' hockey team, while her
grandfather is getting stranger, her father is getting more out
of control, and her best friend, Ben, is ignoring her. (M)

The Gold-Threaded Dress by Carolyn Marsden. Cambridge, MA:
Candlewick Press, 2002. Although Oy is from Thailand, the
students in her fourth grade class call her Chinita, Spanish
for little Chinese. What she wants most is to be accepted by
Lilianda and invited to her club house, and if Oy brings her
traditional Thai dress to school, that might happen.

No Castles Here by A. C. E. Bauer. New York: Random House,
2007. Auggie spends most of his time inside waiting for his
mom to come home from her waitress job. As one of two
white kids in the neighborhood, he tries to be invisible and
avoid the class bully, Dwaine, the other white kid. One day
he catches a train to Philadelphia, goes into a bookstore and

finds a fantasy book that becomes part of the story. (M) (See chapter 3, page 41.)

Nothing Wrong with a Three-Legged Dog by Graham McNamee. New York: Random House, 2000. As the only white kid in his fourth grade class, Keath gets called Whitey, Va-nilla, and Mayonnaise, and his best friend Lynda gets called Zebra because her mom is black and her dad is white.

The Skin I'm In by Sharon G. Flake. New York: Jump at the Sun, 2000. Because Maleeka has dark-black skin and Miss Saunders, the new English teacher, has a white mark over half her face, mean-spirited Charlese doesn't let up on either of them. (M)

Vive La Paris by Esmé Raji Codell. New York: Hyperion Books, 2006. Fifth grader Paris has four older brothers, but only Michael gets physically bullied by Tanaeja, a girl in Paris's class. Michael chooses to follow Martin Luther King's ways to handle her. Meanwhile, Paris has befriended Mrs. Rosen, a Jewish neighbor with a fascinating but painful past.

Yankee Girl by Mary Ann Rodman. New York: Farrar, Straus and Giroux, 2004. It is 1964, and Alice Moxley's dad, an FBI agent, has just been reassigned to Jackson, Mississippi, to cover the integration of public schools. No one in Alice's sixth grade class will talk to her because she is a Yankee, but that is nothing compared to how all the students and teachers treat Valerie Taylor, who integrates Alice's class. The Ku Klux Klan adds another level of harassment by burning its initials in Alice's front lawn and planting a car bomb that kills Valerie's father. (M)

Middle School

The Absolutely True Diary of a Part-Time Indian by Sherman Alexie, illustrated by Ellen Forney. New York: Little, Brown, 2007. Based on his own experiences, Alexie describes a year in the challenging life of Arnold (aka Junior), who loves to draw cartoons, as he deals with tragedies in his family and life in a high school where he is the only Indian.

Bone by Bone by Bone by Tony Johnston. New York: Roaring Brook Press, 2007. In 1950s Tennessee, pre-teenager David's racist father forbids him to play with Malcolm, a black friend, but the boys continue to carry on their special relationship amid racial attacks. (I)

The Boy in the Striped Pajamas by John Boyle. New York: David Flickling Books, 2006. In 1942, nine-year-old Bruno moves with his family to "OutWith," where his father is the new commandant, but no one explains to Bruno about the wire fence outside his bedroom window or the hundreds of people on the other side all shrinking away and wearing striped pajamas. (H)

Day of Tears: A Novel in Dialogue by Julius Lester. New York: Jump at the Sun, 2005. Through a variety of first-person points of view, Lester re-creates a horrendous event in history: the largest slave auction (over four hundred individuals) in America, held in Savannah, Georgia, in 1859. (H)

Devil on My Heels by Joyce McDonald. New York: Delacorte Press, 2004. In a small Florida town in 1959, a white teenage girl sees firsthand the racism and violence the Klan unleashes against black migrant workers in the orange groves. (H)

Face Relations: 11 Stories about Seeing Beyond Color edited by Marilyn Singer. New York: Simon and Schuster, 2004. Stories by Rita Williams-Garcia, Ron Koertge, Joseph Bruchac, Ellen Wittlinger, Kyoko Mori, and others illustrate various racial perspectives.

Gordon Yamamoto and the King of the Geeks by Gene Yang. San Jose: Amazelnk, 2004. Each year, Gordon Yamamoto and Devon pick out the geekiest freshman and humiliate him, and this year's victim is Miles. However, Gordon discovers a Microdroid is stuck in his nose, and Miles is the only one who can help him. After a data transfer between these two, Gordon gains access to all of Miles's memories and realizes he can no longer pick on him. Graphic novel. (I)

House of the Red Fish by Graham Salisbury. New York: Wendy Lamb Books, 2006. In this companion piece to *Under the Blood-Red Sun*, Tomi Nakaji and his friends are determined to raise Tomi's father's sunken fishing sampan from where it was scuttled by the military a year earlier, while trying to deal with a *haole* bully whose racist father controls the lives of Tomi's family. (H)

Koyal Dark, Mango Sweet by Kashmira Sheth. New York: Hyperion Books, 2006. Set in Mumbai, India, this story is about

Jeeta, the youngest, least traditional of three sisters, who may be too dark to marry well. While her mother worries about her marriage prospects, Jeeta looks toward college. (H)

Miguel, Lost and Found in the Palace by Barbara Beasley Murphy. Santa Fe: Museum of New Mexico Press, 2002. Miquel and his family live in El Paso, Texas, where they are harassed because they are Mexicans. The mother and children move to Santa Fe to meet their father; but he has disappeared, and they cannot go to the authorities for help.

Offsides by Erik E. Esckilsen. Boston: Houghton Mifflin, 2004. Refusing to play for a manipulative soccer coach at a high school whose Indian mascot Tom opposes, he forms a rag-tag team that plays against the school's varsity squad in a stunning climax.

Rebound by Bob Krech. Tarrytown, NY: Marshal Cavendish, 2006. All the other Polish guys wrestle but seventeen-year-old Ray Wisniewski just wants to play basketball. In hopes of developing his skills, he joins ROCK, a summer league, where he is one of a few white guys, but discovers that basketball brings him many new friends. Great book for discussion of racism on both the black and white sides but also blacks who stand up for whites and whites who stand up for blacks—standing up for what is just. (H) (See page 106.)

Something about America by Maria Testa. Cambridge, MA: Candlewick Press, 2005. Suffering severe burns when she and her family escaped from Kosova, Albania, the narrator comes to the United States to receive treatment. There is a rally against foreigners, but her father organizes a rally supporting "new Americans." Novel in verse.

Sticks and Stones by Beth Goobie. Victoria, BC: Orca Soundings, 2002. Falsely labeled as a "slut," Jujube fights back against the slurs whispered in the hallways and written on the bathroom walls of her school. (M) (See chapter 2, page 17.)

Under the Same Sky by Cynthia DeFelice. New York: Farrar, Straus and Giroux, 2003. When his dad offers him a job on the family farm, fourteen-year-old Joe Pederson thinks it will be an easy way to earn money for a motorbike. In this coming-of-age story, Joe gains compassion and respect for the Mexican crew he works with, as well as some clarity about his spoiled white friends.

Yellow Line by Sylvia Olsen. Victioria, BC: Orca Book Publishers, 2005. Vince and Sherry have been best friends since they were babies, but now she is dating Steve, an Indian, in a town where whites live on one side of the yellow line in the road and the First Nation lives on the other. And they never mix. (H) (See page 108.)

High School

The Brothers Torres by Coert Voorhees. New York: Hyperion Books, 2008. Frankie has always looked up to his older brother Steve, but now Steve seems on a path contrary to all their family's values in joining the Cholos. As Frankie finds his path, he runs straight into his brother.

Code Talker: A Novel about the Navajo Marines of World War Two by Joseph Bruchac. New York: Dial Books, 2005. An old Navajo describes his experiences as a young boy in a boarding school that repressed his native language, and then what happened when he joined the U.S. military at the age of sixteen and was recruited to become one of the select code talkers to fight in the bloody battles of Bougainville, Guam, Iwo Jima, and Okinawa. (M)

The Confessional by J. L. Powers. New York: Alfred A. Knopf, 2007. After the murder of a student, the all-boy Jesuit High School in El Paso, Texas, has to face the escalating prejudices between the Mexicans, the Mexican-Americans, and the Texas-Americans. (See page 110.)

Eyes of the Emperor by Graham Salisbury. New York: Wendy Lamb Books, 2005. Just before the bombing of Pearl Harbor, a Hawaiian teenager of Japanese ancestry joins the U.S. Army, only to find himself and his Hawaiian comrades discriminated against, and then they are sent to a secret island in Mississippi where they become the bait for training attack dogs. (M)

Generation Dead by Daniel Waters. New York: Hyperion Books, 2008. Adam Layman, the biggest guy on the football team, and Phoebe Kindall, his best friend and goth-girl neighbor, approach their senior year with trepidation as the number of dead kids attending keeps growing. Now, Tommy Williams, a dead kid, has even tried out for football, but the head coach has put out a hit on him! The prejudice in the school and community parallels all the real-life prejudices that exist against minorities. (See chapter 3, page 43.)

The Hoopster by Alan Lawrence Sitomer. New York: Jump at the Sun, 2005. Although he's a hotshot at basketball, Andre wants to be a writer, but his piece about racism in the local newspaper gets him brutally attacked by racists.

Jimi & Me by Jaime Adoff. New York: Hyperion Books, 2005. Biracial eighth grader Keith James and his mother attempt to deal with the death of his beloved father by moving to Hollow Hills, Ohio. In his mourning, Keith dresses in the Jimi Hendrix–era clothing his father left him. That plus his friendship with Veronica, a white girl, makes him a target at his new school. Novel in verse.

Mexican White Boy by Matt de la Peña. New York: Delacorte Press, 2008. Sixteen-year-old Danny does not feel at home in his father's Mexican world or his mother's white world. Before he can live in either, he has to find out who he is.

A Perfect Snow by Nora Martin. New York: Bloomsbury, 2002. Ben Campbell and his family live in a trailer in Logette, Montana, where his father has not been able to find a job. But he has found a church, the Guardians of the Identity, led by Lonn, who believes our problems are almost always someone else's fault. Ben drops out when he realizes the Guardians are a hate group, but his brother doesn't. (See page 112.)

Played by Dana Davidson. New York: Hyperion Books, 2005. Ian Striver, a handsome junior in a large Detroit high school, pledges an underground fraternal group, Freaky Boys Incorporated (FBI). His initiation dictates he must date, seduce, and prove it to the other FBIs—in three weeks. Kylie, the plain girl selected at random, has much to learn—and much to teach as the story unravels.

Thirteen Reasons Why by Jay Asher. New York: Razorbill, 2007. Two weeks ago Hannah Baker committed suicide, but before she did, she made audiotapes explaining her reasons. When the book opens, Clay Jensen is listening to the tapes. These two voices narrate the story giving the reader a full picture of all that happened to Hannah since ninth grade. One of the first authors to deal with bullycide, Asher gives the reader a thorough analysis of sexual harassment, from a few hurtful words to destructive actions Hannah cannot escape. (See chapter 9, page 177.)

Who Will Tell My Brother by Marlene Carvell. New York: Hyperion Books, 2002. Though Evan has always been conscious of his Mohawk heritage, it is not until his senior year in high school that he feels the need to take a stand by asking the school board to change the offensive Indian school mascot. Though his attempts are quiet and follow the established recourse, the harassment he suffers ranges from personal verbal attacks to violence against his whole family. (M)

7

Homophobia: That's So Gay!

I had just given my sophomore students their homework assignment when I heard a voice from somewhere in the room moan, "Oh Ms. Bott, that's so gay!" I stopped, looking puzzled. "You're telling me the homework assignment is gay?" Several heads nodded. I acted surprised. "What about my assignment is homosexual?" "No!" the whole class groaned, except for those who could not believe I had said the word "homosexual." Eventually, a student courageously, and thoughtlessly, in my mind, said, "No, we just mean it's stupid."

In that teachable moment, the homework assignment, stupid or otherwise, was forgotten.

The phrase "That's so gay" entered our language around 2000, and it is still being used today as I write this. On October 3, 2008, I googled "That's so gay" and found 623,000 links on the Internet. On the Gay, Lesbian and Straight Education Network (GLSEN) website, Nancy Goldstein asserts "That's so gay" has become the put-down du jour in schools nationwide and "faggot" the ultimate insult for male students.[1] These expressions are not fading away as so many slang phrases do.

On March 18, 2008, *BBC News Magazine* posted an article titled "How 'Gay' Became the Children's Insult of Choice" by Denise Winterman, reporting that according to a survey by the Association of Teachers and Lecturers, 83 percent of the teachers interviewed said "gay" is now the most frequently used term of abuse in schools.

Winterman quotes psychologist Ian Rivers in reference to the label "gay": "'It's not about your heritage or your race, it's not about things which someone can see.' So it can't even be challenged, he says. 'How can children demonstrate that they are heterosexual? There's no effective recourse and this is what makes it so effective as a bullying tactic.'"[2]

"Gay" is an easy word to throw at someone. Young kids use it without knowing what it means, and young adults use it knowing exactly what it means. What may start as name-calling in early elementary school quickly becomes hate talk by middle school and can grow into hate crimes later. As educators, we hear it all the time and rarely confront it.

Dealing with the topic of homophobia (an irrational hatred, disapproval, or fear of homosexuality, gay and lesbian people, and their culture) is difficult for teachers for many reasons. That day in my class, what supported me was an Acceptance poster that hung in my classroom and every classroom in our school that pledged acceptance of everyone. That document gave me permission to discuss many topics I might not have attempted if I did not know where our school system stood. If our administration could commit to this acceptance of everyone, I insisted on supporting it in my classroom. It still bothers me that as a starting teacher I was afraid of saying or doing the wrong thing and getting myself fired. I know I became a much better teacher when I didn't have to be afraid to support all my students, when I did not have to pretend I had not heard or seen something that humiliated someone. If your school does not have such a policy, there are many sample policies available on the Internet, and adapting one for your school will promote ownership with the staff. One of the many available resources is GLSEN (www.glsen.org); on its website you will find the article "Frequently Asked Questions on Safe School Policies," which will answer many of your questions.

Gay students are not only harassed by students, they are also abandoned by most staff members who do not act when they witness bullying or harassment. Though we may feel more comfortable disciplining someone who shoves a handicapped child or takes someone's lunch money, we are often quiet after witnessing other bullying events. Many of us are uncomfortable when we witness homophobic harassment, and that feeling and our ignorance make it easier to ignore the event. The problem is that when a staff member ignores a racial, sexual, or homophobic slur, that silence supports it. The bully/harasser, the targeted student, and everyone watching that event believe the adult sides with the bully. Teachers and staff have the right to believe as they choose, but we are required by law to keep all of our students safe.

The books in this chapter will help open the discussion. Many of the picture books show families that are different from the traditional model—father, mother, and children. Learning at an early age that not all families have the same ingredients makes everyone's family less different and spreads acceptance. There are many children in our country being raised by grandparents, usually a grandmother, or children with only one parent, or an older sibling acting as a parent. And there are children who have two mommies or daddies. All of these family models need to be validated. The picture book *And Tango Makes Three* by Justin Richardson and Peter Parnel tells the story of a penguin family in New York's Central Park with two daddies. *All Families Are Special* by Norma Simon and *The Family Book* by Todd Parr are two more of the many picture books that speak to this theme.

Middle school and high school books focus on different approaches in exposing homophobia. *Between Mom and Jo* by Julie Anne Peters is told from the perspective of Nick, a fourteen-year-old boy who remembers the harassment he faced growing up with two moms. In *Crossover* by Jeff Rud, Kyle Evans realizes that his hidden homophobia may have been the reason he distanced himself from his middle school friend Lucas. In high school, Kyle rethinks his behavior. Carlos Amoroso, in Alex Sanchez's *Getting It*, realizes that if he ever wants to talk to Roxy Rodriguez he will need a coach, so he asks Sal, the gay guy at school who talks with all the girls, to give him some pointers, but Carlos's friends react with homophobic comments.

Books for teens no longer only present plots where the gay character is physically beaten and killed; the authors and their audience have grown and humor has been introduced. In *Absolutely Positively Not*, Steven works very hard at not being gay. He plasters women's lingerie ads all over his room, tries to sit with the football players at lunch, and has twenty-eight dates in twenty-six days. But when he finally shares with his best friend that he may be gay, she hugs him and says, "Finally."

Authors continue to challenge the taboos. *Evolution, Me & Other Freaks of Nature* by Robin Brande; *The God Box* by Alex Sanchez; and *Nothing Pink* by Mark Hardy confront the issue of homosexuality and religion. In *Evolution*, when Mena Reese supports a gay friend, their Christian friends ostracize them both. In *The God Box*, Paul works very hard to maintain his relationship with Jesus, which becomes more confusing when he meets Manuel, an openly gay Christian. In *Nothing Pink*, Vincent knows he is damned to hell by his church and his preacher father; but no matter how hard he prays, God does not change him.

Hopefully the next time you hear the phrase "That's so gay," these books will have prepared you for that teachable moment.

FOCUS BOOKS

Picture Books

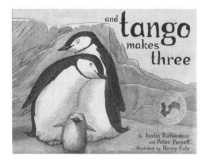

And Tango Makes Three by Justin Richardson and Peter Parnell, illustrated by Henry Cole. New York: Simon and Schuster, 2005.

Roy and Silo watched how the other penguins made a home. So they built a nest of stones for themselves.

New York City has a big park filled with lots of things for children to do, including a zoo filled with animal families. In the penguin house, there are lots of penguin families. Roy and Silo are both boys, but they are best friends and do everything together. When the other penguin families build nests with stones, Roy and Silo build one too. But when the mamas lay eggs that will hatch into baby penguins, Roy and Silo can only watch. One day Mr. Gramzay, the penguin keeper, discovers an egg without a family, and he puts it in Roy and Silo's nest. They take very good care of the egg and when it hatches, Mr. Gramzay names the baby penguin Tango. Roy and Silo and Tango make a very happy family.

Topics for Discussion

1. Have you ever been to a zoo? Have you ever seen a penguin?
2. What do penguins use to build their nests?
3. Roy and Silo are best friends. What are some things they do together as best friends? What do you and your best friend do together?
4. When they didn't have an egg to sit on, what did they use instead?
5. How does Mr. Gramzay help them to become a family?

Quotes for Reader Response

- Everyday families of all kinds go to visit the animals that live there.
- Roy and Silo were both boys. But they did everything together.
- Roy and Silo knew just what to do. They moved the egg to the center of their nest. Every day they turned it, so each side stayed warm.
- Roy and Silo taught Tango how to sing for them when she was hungry.
- And all the children who came to the zoo could see Tango and her two fathers playing in the penguin house with the other penguins.

Molly's Family by Nancy Garden, illustrated by Sharon Wooding. New York: Farrar, Straus and Giroux, 2004.

> *Tommy laughed. "Molly says she has a mommy and a mama," he told everyone. "But there's no such thing."*

Ms. Marston asks her kindergarten students to help prepare the room for Open School Night; some clean and dust, and some draw pictures. Molly draws a picture of her family, her Mommy, her Mama Lu, and Sam, her puppy. But Tommy doesn't believe anyone can have two mommies. Ms. Marston handles the situation nicely.

Topics for Discussion

1. Name all the people in your family.
2. Do all families have to be the same? Is it even possible for all families to be the same?
3. What is one special thing about your family?
4. How did Molly get two mommies?

Quotes for Reader Response

- Tommy looked at Molly's paper. "That's not a family," he said.
- "But you don't have to have a daddy. I [Stephen] don't have a daddy."
- There were different kinds of families in her very own class!
- That evening all the families came—even Tommy's and Molly's puppies!

Intermediate

I could not find any intermediate books that deal with homophobia. I suggest checking titles from the picture book and the middle school sections.

Middle School

Between Mom and Jo by Julie Anne Peters. New York: Little, Brown, 2006.

After parents' night I started getting all A's on my paper; even when I missed answers. Even when I missed them on purpose. There are lots of different ways of taking it out on people, like making them feel they don't even exist. (50)

Told through flashbacks and supplemented with notes from his current fourteen-year-old self, Nicholas Nathaniel Thomas Tucker relives the years from his third birthday to the present with his two mothers. The harassment starts in kindergarten when the boys ask about his pervert mothers and label him Dickless Nicholas, and it doesn't stop. Nick learns to ignore it and never brings it home. That would just upset his two moms—Erin, his biological mother, and Jo, his heart's mother. There are other problems in their family. Jo battles alcoholism, Erin is diagnosed with breast cancer, they break up, and Erin starts a new relationship with Kerri. Nick, feeling abandoned and discarded, plunges into despair. More than just the story of a boy with two mothers, this is the story of a family that goes through many of life's hardships, including a divorce. In that way, it parallels many families that lose the bonds that made them a family.

Topics for Discussion

1. How are Nick's two moms, Erin and Jo, different?
2. Explain the difference in the relationships Nick has with his moms.
3. Identify at least three examples of homophobia that hurt Nick.
4. Mrs. Ivey, his teacher, made Nick feel invisible in several ways. List at least three of those ways.
5. How does Nick react to the bullies? Why doesn't he tell his moms?
6. Children are often told to go to an understanding adult when bullying happens. Is there any adult other than his mothers that Nick could go to?

7. Is there anything in the book that reminds you of your life? (I remember my dad and I used to spit watermelon seeds.)
8. Why does Nick want to live with Jo?
9. Kerri sneaked Nick out to see Jo. Why did she do that?
10. How does Nick finally convince Erin that he needs to live with Jo?

Quotes for Reader Response

- The guy's eyes bore into mine. "That's right, Nicky," he went. "Your moms are freaks. And so are you. Dickless Nicholas. Hey, that's a good one." (24)
- Jo cocks her head at Mrs. Ivey. "Where's Nick's picture?" Mrs. Ivey's face jiggles. "I . . . I must've missed it. Let me look through my desk." (47)
- When I tell Mom and Jo what Jessica said . . . No, I won't tell. It happens all the time now, the slurs, the stares, the laughing behind our backs. I never tell. (56)
- Who cares what people say? I love my moms. (57)
- Ever since kindergarten and "Dickless Nicholas," I'd pretty much learned to live with the bashing. Calling my moms "dykes" and "homos" and "lesbos" was one thing, but Josh crossed the line when he said they were going to burn in hell. (60)
- This is it. My Defining Moment. That's what Jo calls it. The one memory that stays freshest in your mind and marks a turning point. The moment in time that characterizes what your life will be about. (85)
- "She asked me to tell you. She just—" Jo stops and swallows hard. "She couldn't." She exhales a shallow breath. "Her surgery is Monday morning, Nick. If you want to ditch tomorrow, you're allowed." Jo turns and forces a smile. "I am."
  I think, I'll never go back to school. I'm never leaving this house. I'll never, ever let either of them out of my sight again. (91)
- Mom straightens and sighs. "Sit down, Nick. I need to tell you something." My hear rips. A black hole opens up. My

first thought, my only thought is, No. "Jo left," she says. "We split up." (130)

- "You're my birth mom. I know that. I *get* that." I open my eyes. "But Jo . . ." I hesitate because I don't know how Mom's going to react to this. She has to know, though. Deep in her heart I think she does, and that's the problem. That's what makes it so hard to say. "Jo's my real mom." (204)

orca sports

Crossover

Jeff Rud

Crossover by Jeff Rud. Victoria, BC: Orca Sports, 2008.

> *Homophobia! I hadn't really thought about it clearly until now, but I knew he was right. That's exactly what this was— the fear or hatred of gay people. (113)*

Junior Kyle Evans has two talents: one is on the basketball court, where he has just made senior squad and starter, and the other is on stage. He hasn't been involved with theater since middle school, but this year the high school fall production is *Oliver*. Kyle's girlfriend, Jenna McBride, and his old friend Lukas Connor try to convince Kyle to try out with them. Coach Williams wants Kyle to quit the play, and Ben Stillman, the coach's six-foot-five, two-hundred-pound favorite, starts pushing his own homophobic agenda with the help of his two thugs, Kurt and Joey. These three trash the play's sets, covering them with homophobic slurs.

Kyle and Lukas renew their former friendship, while Ben increases his taunting and gay bashing. Kyle starts to examine why he had distanced himself from Lukas after middle school and wonders if he is homophobic.

The homophobia in the book is typical in schools, and the honesty between Kyle and Lukas will lead to discussions about the role of a responsible friend and show that Kyle's willingness to talk about feelings and to apologize for avoiding Lukas can strengthen the friendship and decrease the power of homophobia.

Topics for Discussion

1. One way that Ben bullies is by calling people names. List the words he uses to target Kyle, Lukas, and others he bullies.
2. When Lukas first asks Kyle to try out for the play, how does Kyle react? Later he questions his behavior. What does he realize?
3. What made Ben the coach's favorite? How does Coach Williams's favoritism affect the team?
4. What are examples that the coach might be homophobic?
5. Why did Ben, Kurt, and Joey destroy the set for *Oliver*?
6. Both the principal and the coach ask for help in identifying the vandals. Why didn't anyone speak up?
7. If you knew who the vandals were, what would you do?
8. On page 131, Lukas asks, "Why would anybody do something like that to my locker?" Answer his question.
9. Why does Jenna feel so strongly that Kyle needs to tell the principal what he knows about the vandalism?
10. Have you ever avoided or not done the right thing?
11. How does your school handle homophobia?

Quotes for Reader Response

- Lukas was all right. But he wasn't like the rest of my friends. He was shy. He didn't like sports. He was a little on the feminine side. He didn't really fit into my crowd. (22)
- "Nice to see you ladies all here on time," Coach Williams said sarcastically. (23)
- "Obviously, you're not quitting hoops. But I don't get why you want to hang with all those theater geeks anyway." (85)
- "I thought you were supposed to be a basketball player, not one of the funny boys of the drama department." (92)

- I felt horrible for Lukas. I'd never really realized that people had such a problem with him. And I didn't really understand it. What did it matter if he was different? (105)
- I had heard all the terms—gay, homo, queer, queen, fag. I had even used them once or twice myself. But until this morning, I hadn't thought about what those words actually meant or how hurtful they could be. I was ashamed of myself for not realizing that before. (108)
- I hadn't bullied or teased Lukas like Ben Stillman and his buddies had, but I had never stepped up to stop it, either. (116)
- I also couldn't help but think about all the times my basketball teammates and I had used the words *gay* and *fag* and *queer*. We hadn't meant that stuff to be hateful—I hadn't, anyway—but that's what it was. (121)
- "Kyle," Jenna said firmly, "you've got to stop worrying so much about what other people think. You have to figure out what's the right thing to do and do it." (147)

High School

The God Box by Alex Sanchez. New York: Simon and Schuster, 2007.

> *I think that unless people are told to believe homosexuality and God are in conflict, there is no conflict. (171)*

Paul Mendoza doesn't like to attract attention and goes by Paul instead of his birth name, Pablo, so he will better fit in. His family is a spiritual family: his father found Alcoholic Anonymous through their Baptist minister; his abuelita has a running conversation with God; and when something troubles

Paul, he prays, writes down the problem, and puts it in his God Box. He and his girlfriend, Angie, are part of the Christ on Campus Bible Club. What no one but Jesus knows is that Paul carries two conflicts inside him: he believes he may be gay, and if he is, his Baptist Church and the Bible say he is an abomination and will burn in hell.

On the first day of school, a new student, Manuel, joins their lunch table. When they ask, he answers their questions: yes he is Christian, and yes he is gay. Paul sits frozen. "Didn't he realize the consequences of what he was saying? Students would shun and ridicule him—or worse" (5). Before long Angie fights to start a Gay Straight Alliance (GSA), while the biggest homophobes in the building are getting vicious.

During the book, Paul does everything he believes Jesus wants him to do, including talking with his minister and meeting with a man from an ex-gay ministry. Manuel knows the Bible better than the minister, and his interpretations make sense to Paul. Listening to every argument on both sides about homosexuality, Paul feels like a battlefield by the time he finds his place in life.

Topics for Discussion

1. List three people in the book who are honest about their beliefs and display consistency in their thoughts and actions.
2. Would you consider Paul to be a good person?
3. Explain the difference between Jude Maldonado's homophobia and Elizabeth's homophobia.
4. How are they each a danger to Manuel?
5. What other types of homophobic thinking are displayed in the book?
6. Why does Angie have such a difficult time getting a sponsor for the new GSA?
7. Paul's abuelita has not always had an easy life. Explain her faith and her acceptance of homosexuality.
8. In the beginning of the book, what does Paul believe God says about his being gay? What does Manuel believe God says about his being gay?

9. What do you believe about someone being gay? How do you treat a gay person?
10. Of all the Bible verses quoted, which holds the most meaning in your life, or what quote outside of the Bible holds meaning in your life?

Quotations for Reader Response

- Then Elizabeth asked, "Are you a Christian?" "Some days more than others." Manuel gave a relaxed grin, "But I try to be." (4)
- "So . . ." Dakota, intrepid journalist and always to the point, leaned toward Manuel. "Are *you* gay?" I expected him to laugh or get angry, but he calmly twirled his spaghetti noodles. "Yep." (5)
- Sometimes it seems that if you looked hard enough, you could find a Bible verse to justify anything. (26–27)
- Jude Maldonado announced to one of his buddies: "If I saw two guys walk down the street holding hands, I'd take a baseball bat and kill them." (34)
- Most of all I loved the church for bringing Jesus into my heart. (46)
- "After today's Bible study," Angie explained, "we think we need to do something before somebody gets killed. So we're going to start a GA. We want you to help us." (87)
- Jude has begun making life hell for Manuel in any and every way he could: spitting on his seat in class, bodychecking him in the hallway, or "accidentally" squirting him with ketchup at lunchtime. Even though the teachers and lunch patrol saw what was happening (they'd have been blind not to), none of them did anything to stop it. (135)
- What would it be like to feel free, to not be hiding from anyone? (166)
- But when Pa reached the aisle, he stopped and drew himself up. My pa, who hated speaking in front of even small groups, said in a voice loud enough for all to hear. "Pastor, you're wrong." (221)
- After all my prayers for change, uttered and stuffed into my little box, God did change me—just not the way I'd wanted.

I still don't understand why I'm gay, but now I accept what I always knew inside my heart: It's just how I am. (247)

In the Garage by Alma Fullerton. Calgary: Red Deer Press, 2006.

There'll always be shit that happens in your life that'll make you wonder what the hell God was thinking when he made humans. (8)

The book opens at Alex's funeral. BJ stands to give the eulogy and is filled with the eight years of memories from their friendship and confusion of how they got to this day. Those flashbacks, revealed through BJ's narration and poetry from Alex's journal, tell the story.

When BJ was a little kid, her mother yelled, "I can't stand to look at your ugly face anymore." Then she left BJ locked in a car in a public parking lot and walked away—forever. Her grandmother, Nan, and her father are able to create a loving home, but BJ never forgets that moment. School is enemy territory, as many students are no more accepting than her mother and the chants of "Ugly, ugly, ugly" pierce her heart.

Then in third grade, in the middle of an attack by fifth grade boys, New Kid jumps in, confronts the bullies, and becomes BJ's friend. The world starts to change, but maybe she can't trust it. On her eighth birthday, her father, Nan, and Alex—no longer New Kid—buy her a video camera so she can document everything. On Alex's tenth birthday, BJ uses all her birthday money to buy him the guitar that he wants but that his father refuses to buy. They have given each other an escape.

Alex lives with a secret even BJ doesn't know. His journal shows his self-doubts and fear of disappointing his dad and not being able to meet his dad's expectations. He also struggles with a growing awareness that he may be gay. He wants to tell BJ but never does—he just puts everything in his journal.

Both BJ and Alex are different. BJ's difference and her betrayal of Alex force her to seriously harm herself. Her betrayal releases Alex's secret and incites a homophobic mob that kills him.

Topics for Discussion

1. What would have happened in BJ's life if Alex had never moved to town?
2. BJ and Alex give each other very important gifts. What were they and why were they so special?
3. What made BJ vulnerable to Victoria and Rachel?
4. What did Victoria and Rachel want from BJ?
5. Alex's father is only in the book through Alex's thoughts. What does Alex believe are his father's goals for him?
6. What was Alex's fear concerning his father? Do you think that fear was realistic?
7. List all the examples of the homophobia in this book.
8. Before his journal is exposed, what is Alex's reputation around school?
9. Did that reputation help him in the end? Isn't that what BJ was trying to tell the mob in the garage?
10. When Rick and the mob get to the garage, what was their plan?
11. Are we judged more by our actions or by the labels others put on us?
12. How can anyone protect himself or herself from rumors?

Quotes for Reader Response

- They're staring at *me*, at my scar, at my blotch, picking out all that's wrong with me, and I'm numb. (11)
- Tormented / by what I am, / and confronted by / what I want to be. (13)
- "Ugly, ugly, ugly!" It's third grade and Brian and Darren— fifth grade Booger-Bullies—push me around. Their jackets swing as they shove me between each other, back and forth, back and forth. (21)

- The note says, *Alex only likes you because he wants to work for the humane society.* (30)
- BJ knows me so well, / I'm afraid sometimes / she can look deep into my eyes / and see my whole life is an act. (35)
- It's not me they hate anymore. It's Alex—and it's all my fault. (120)
- I take the wire hairbrush out of my backpack. I bring that wire brush up to my face, up to my blotch. And I try to scrape that blotch off the face of the girl I no longer recognize. (122)
- In real life there are no second chances to tell people what you need to tell them. No second chances to say sorry. In real life once you're dead, you're dead. (140)
- BJ is yelling, "That's Alex!" BJ is screaming over the cries of the angry mob. "He's still Alex!" BJ is clawing at their faces, trying to get them off of me. She's screaming "He's still the same kid we all grew up with! He's still Alex." (178–79)
- "Alex was *home* to us and we should have been *home* to him. We should have made him feel like we'd accept him for him—no matter who he was inside." (180)

ANNOTATED BIBLIOGRAPHY

Some books are appropriate for other levels; I = intermediate grades, M = middle school, H = high school. Books discussed at length elsewhere in this text are noted parenthetically.

Picture Books

All Families Are Special by Norma Simon, illustrated by Teresa Flavin. Morton Grove, IL: Albert Whitman, 2003. After Mrs. Mack announces she will soon be a grandmother, she and her students talk about their families and realize how many different types of families there are.

And Tango Makes Three by Justin Richardson and Peter Parnell, illustrated by Henry Cole. New York: Simon and Schuster, 2005. In New York's Central Park Zoo, there are two male penguins who hatch an egg and raise the baby penguin as their own. (See page 128.)

The Daddy Machine by Johnny Valentine, illustrated by Lynette Schmidt. 2nd ed. Los Angeles: Alyson Wonderland, 2004. Two sisters live in a house with their cat, their parakeet, and their two moms. One day their moms have to work on the same day and leave a big gift for the girls, who use all the contained levers, gears, pulleys, and bolts to build a Daddy Machine, which produces not one Daddy but sixty-three!

The Different Dragon by Jennifer Bryan, illustrated by Danamarie Hosler. Ridley Park, PA: Two Lives, 2006. Noah, washed and ready for bed, asks Go-Ma, one of his two mothers, to tell him a story. With Noah's help, Go-Ma takes them on a wonderful and wise visit to a dragon who doesn't want to be what everyone expects him to be—fierce.

"The Duke Who Outlawed Jelly Beans" and Other Stories by Johnny Valentine, illustrated by Lynette Schmidt. Los Angeles: Alyson Wonderland, 1991. This fun fairytale collection has five stories, each containing at least one secondary character who is gay.

Emma and Meesha My Boy: A Two Mom Story by Kaitlyn Considine, illustrated by Binny Hobbs. West Hartford, CT: Twomombooks.com, 2005. Emma treats her cat, Meesha, like a toy until her two moms help her learn the best way to care for a cat.

The Family Book by Todd Parr. New York: Little, Brown, 2003. Using human and animal families displayed through colorful graphics, Parr writes about ways families are different and alike.

King & King by Linda de Haan and Stern Nijland. Berkeley: Tricycle Press, 2000. The queen is tired of being the queen and wants her son to marry and take over the throne. The prince shows no interest until he meets Princess Madeleine's brother, Prince Lee.

Mini Mia and Her Darling Uncle by Pija Lindenbaum, translated by Elisabeth Kallick Dyssegaard. Stockholm, Sweden: Raben and Sjogren Books, distributed by Farrar, Straus and Giroux (New York), 2007. Tommy is Mini Mia's favorite uncle and they have wonderful times together. Then one day she meets

Fergus and discovers she has to share Uncle Tommy with him! Mini Mia fights that idea for a long time, until she discovers Fergus can play soccer really well.

Molly's Family by Nancy Garden, illustrated by Sharon Wooding. New York: Farrar, Straus and Giroux, 2004. When Molly draws a picture of her family for Open School Night, the fact that she has two moms confuses Tommy. (See page 129.)

The Sissy Duckling by Harvey Fierstein, illustrated by Henry Cole. New York: Aladdin Paperbacks, 2002. After big bully Drake chases Elmer away from school because he is just too different, and Elmer's father calls him a sissy, Elmer runs away and makes a home in a hollow tree. When the hunters start shooting, Elmer bravely saves his father.

Uncle Bobby's Wedding by Sarah S. Brannen. New York: G. P. Putnam's Sons, 2008. Chloe doesn't want her favorite uncle to get married; she likes having all his attention. When she meets Jamie, she likes him so much she even helps plan the wedding. All the characters are guinea pigs.

Intermediate

I could not find any intermediate books that deal with homophobia.

Middle School

Between Mom and Jo by Julie Anne Peters. New York: Little, Brown and Company, 2006. Fourteen-year-old Nick introduces himself in memories that tell the story of his life with his two lesbian moms: Erin, his biological mother, and Jo, his heart's mother. (H) (See page 130.)

Crossover by Jeff Rud. Victoria, BC: Orca Sports, 2008. Kyle Evans loves basketball, but he also loves theater and this year the fall production is *Oliver*. After he gets a part, he has to deal with an angry coach and a homophobic teammate who sets out to destroy him and Lukas, a perceived-to-be-gay cast member. (See page 133.)

Death by Eggplant by Susan Heyboer O'Keefe. Brookfield, CT: Roaring Brook Press, 2004. Bertie Hooks spends his days planning new recipes and ducking his tormentor, Nick Dekker, until his math teacher gives him an assignment in responsibility. A hilarious book and the homophobia is subtle.

Evolution, Me & Other Freaks of Nature by Robin Brande. New York: Alfred A. Knopf, 2007. Mena Reese enters ninth grade ostracized by all her former Christian friends because she could not support their harassment of a perceived-to-be-gay student, Danny Pierce, who moved away. This year's conflict is the evolution versus intelligent design debate, and the complications keep multiplying. (H)

Men of Stone by Gayle Friesen. Toronto: Kids Can Press, 2000. Fifteen-year-old Ben had a strong interest in dance but gave it up because he was tired of the harassment. Claude's bullying is escalating, and Ben takes up boxing as a way to survive. (H)

The Misfits by James Howe. New York: Atheneum, 2001. Four social outcasts in seventh grade create a third political party and run for student council on a "No Name-Calling" platform. (See chapter 2, page 12.)

Pretty Tough by Liz Tigelaar. New York: Razorbill, 2007. Charlie Brown, sophomore, has been an outcast since her best friend, Regan Holder, turned on her last year and spread rumors that Charlie was lesbian. Charlie's sister Krista, older by two years, supported Regan's rumors with her silence.

So Hard to Say by Alex Sanchez. New York: Simon and Schuster, 2004. New to the school, eighth grader Frederick starts playing soccer with the other boys after school and questions his attraction to one of them. The treasure of diversity in this book deals with the needed acceptance of one's self and others.

Totally Joe by James Howe. New York: Atheneum, 2005. Joe Bunch, one of the gang from *The Misfits*, writes about his life, focusing on his admission to himself, his family, and his schoolmates that he is gay in an alphabiography for school.

The Truth about Truman School by Dori Hillestad Butler, Morton Grove, IL: Albert Whitman, 2008. Homophobia is secondary to cyberbullying in this story about two eighth graders who create an Internet newspaper where students can post the truth about their school. (See chapter 8, page 154.)

High School

Absolutely Positively Not by David Larochelle. New York: Arthur A. Levine, 2005. Steven does NOT want to be gay. He hangs girlie pictures all over his bedroom, has twenty-eight dates in twenty-six days, and tries to invade the football players' table in the lunch room. But still under his bed, wrapped in rubber bands and locked in a suitcase covered with an old blanket, he has two men's underwear catalogs.

Alt Ed by Catherine Atkins. New York: G. P. Putnam's Sons, 2003. Susan Callaway, an overweight, silent tenth grader, is assigned Alt Ed, an alternative-to-suspension program with six other students. One is Kale, the biggest bully in school, and another is Brendan, who is perceived to be gay and Kale's main target.

Boy Girl Boy by Ron Koertge. New York: Harcourt, 2005. Tired of their small town lives and their oddball parents, good friends Elliot, Teresa, and Larry plan to leave town the day after graduation, but after Larry is badly beaten by the local bully/homophobe, their plans change.

Debbie Harry Sings in French by Meagan Brothers. New York: Henry Holt, 2008. Johnny escapes the harsh realities of a father who died in a car crash that also killed others and a mother who copes with the loss by immersion in alcohol. Johnny saves himself with a love of music, but later his own descent into drugs and alcohol causes his mother to send him to a private school near his uncle in South Carolina. Though he finds a girlfriend there, the cool boys label him a faggot.

Eight Seconds by Jean Ferris. New York: Harcourt, 2000. After his dad signs him up for rodeo camp, John finds a competition he's good at—riding bulls. That's easy compared to the friendship he has formed with his rodeo buddy, Kit, who is gay.

Far from Xanadu by Julie Anne Peters. New York: Little, Brown, 2005. After Mike's father commits suicide, life changes drastically for Mike, her deeply depressed mother, and her older brother. Then bad girl Xanadu moves to town, and even though Mike isn't sure about her own sexuality, she falls in love with Xanadu.

Finding H. F. by Julia Watts. Los Angeles: Alyson Books, 2001. H. F. (Heavenly Faith) and Bo (Pierre Beauregard) are trying to survive in Morgan, Kentucky, where H. F. says, "It may be hard for a tomboy but it is way harder for a sissy boy." On a road trip to find H. F.'s mother, they discover they aren't the only gay kids in America.

Freak Show by James St. James. New York: Dutton Children's Books, 2007. Billy Bloom lives life in drag, and when his fashion outdoes his mother's, she sends him from their home in New York City to his father in the Everglades. From his first day at Dwight D. Eisenhower Academy, his over-the-top outfits make him a target. Even after a mob beating that hospitalizes him for weeks, Billy doesn't give up—in fact, he runs for homecoming queen!

The Full Spectrum: A New Generation of Writing about Gay, Lesbian, Bisexual, Transgender, Questioning, and Other Identities edited by David Levithan and Billy Merrell. New York: Alfred A. Knopf, 2006. Forty people share their personal stories about accepting their sexual identities. Nonfiction.

Gay, Lesbian, and Transgender Issues in Education: Programs, Policies, and Practices edited by James T. Sears. New York: Hayworth Press, 2005. The structure of this book—chapters written by different authors on topics related to gay, lesbian, and transgender issues and then commentaries by other professionals and the authors' reactions—keeps it centered and yet offers several voices. A helpful book for questioning teens as it gives a view of this issue in several countries around the world and for adults who do not yet understand the isolation experienced. Nonfiction.

Getting It by Alex Sanchez. New York: Simon and Schuster, 2006. Carlos Amoroso doesn't have the confidence to talk to Roxy Rodriguez, but he notices Sal, the gay guy at school, has no trouble talking to girls. Inspired by TV's *Queer Eye*, Carlos asks Sal for some help. A nice friendship follows that confuses Carlos's other friends.

GLBTQ: The Survival Guide for Queer & Questioning Teens by Kelly Huegel. Minneapolis: Free Spirit, 2003. With extensive research, useful information, accessible language, and resources for the Gay, Lesbian, Bisexual, Transgender, and Questioning Teen, this book seems to cover everything. (M)

The God Box by Alex Sanchez. New York: Simon and Schuster, 2007. Paul, a born-again Christian, works very hard to maintain his relationship with Jesus; but on the first day of school, transfer student Manuel's announcement that he is Christian and gay triggers Paul's confusion about his own sexuality. Bible verses fill this book. (See page 135.)

grl2grl by Julie Anne Peters. New York: Little, Brown, 2007. In ten emotional short stories, Peters explores the experiences of lesbian and transgendered teenagers—some tough, others vulnerable—as they search for love, acceptance, and identity.

Hear Us Out! Lesbian and Gay Stories of Struggle, Progress, and Hope, 1950 to the Present by Nancy Garden. New York: Farrar, Straus and Giroux, 2007. Garden does a superb job of summarizing the history of gay experiences during each decade and follows each of those six nonfiction sections with two short stories about teenagers that illustrate those times. (M)

The Heart Has Its Reasons: Young Adult Literature with Gay/ Lesbian/Queer Content, 1969–2004 by Michael Cart and Christine A. Jenkins. Lanham, MD: Scarecrow Press, 2006. This history of young adult literature's slow inclusion of books with gay/lesbian/queer characters begins in 1969. The text discusses the sociological climate through the decades and includes an annotated bibliography for each decade.

In the Garage by Alma Fullerton. Calgary: Red Deer Press, 2006. BJ and Alex had been best friends for eight years, but Alex couldn't share his most private secret with her. Told in flashbacks by BJ while at Alex's funeral. (M) (See page 138.)

Keeping You a Secret by Julie Anne Peters, New York: Little, Brown, 2003. Holland, one of the leaders of her senior class, is confident nothing could shake her from this earned position, but then she falls in love with Cece, a new girl at school.

The Last Exit to Normal by Michael Harmon. New York: Alfred A. Knopf, 2008. Ben Campbell, at fourteen, had a pretty normal life until his father announces he is gay, his mother leaves the family, and his father's new partner moves in. At seventeen, Ben is acting out and as a result, the family moves from Washington to Montana, where Ben meets Ron Jamison, the most troubled and violent kid in town.

Luna by Julie Anne Peters. New York: Little, Brown, 2004. Regan and Liam share a secret that most brothers and sisters don't have: deep down inside, Liam is really a girl named Luna, and Luna needs to be freed.

Nothing Pink by Mark Hardy. Ashville: Front Street, 2008. Based on what his church and his preacher father have told him, fourteen-year-old Vincent knows he is damned to hell for being gay even though he has never even held hands with another boy. Not until Vince deals directly with God does he feel at peace with himself. (M)

Parrotfish by Ellen Wittlinger. New York: Simon and Schuster, 2007. When Angela goes to school on Monday, she will no longer be Angela; she will be Grady, a male. Grady hopes the new non-gender-specific name will make the transition easier. Set around Christmas time, the book contains humor that helps balance the intensity of Grady's new life. (M)

A Really Nice Prom Mess by Brian Sloan. New York: Simon and Schuster, 2005. Cameron Hayes and his partner, Shane, decide to take girls to their high school prom, but hilarious mishaps lead to adventures all over town. It is difficult to find a funny book on this topic.

7 Days at the Hot Corner by Terry Trueman. New York: Harper-Tempest, 2007. Baseball is the most important thing in Scott's life, especially now that his high school team is competing for the state championship, and he hopes to show everyone that he's good enough to play professional baseball. But his discovery that his best friend is gay gives him a lot more to be concerned about.

Tips on Having a Gay (ex) Boyfriend by Carrie Jones. Woodbury, MN: Flux, 2007. Seniors Belle and Dylan have been a couple, best friends, and lovers for years—but though Dylan still loves Belle, he accepts that he is gay. The homophobia in the book takes on different forms, some a defensive reaction for Belle, who is the only person who still stands up for Dylan.

What Happened to Lani Garver by Carol Plum-Ucci. New York: Harcourt, 2002. Claire McKenzie tells the story of her friend Lani Garver's brief stay on Hackett Island, where most of the island is trying to decide if Lani is a he or a she. Told in flashbacks, Lani, wise, sensitive, and courageous, died at the hand of the island's rednecks before the book opens.

NOTES

1. Nancy Goldstein, "Zero Indifference: A How-to Guide to Ending Name-Calling in Schools," GLSEN, November 2, 2001, www.glsen.org/cgi-bin/iowa/all/news/record/850.html (accessed October 29, 2008).

2. Denise Winterman, "How 'Gay' Became the Children's Insult of Choice," *BBC News Magazine*, March 18, 2008, http://news.bbc.co.uk/2/hi/uk_news/magazine/7289390.stm (accessed October 29, 2008).

8

Cyberbullying and Cyberspace

Imagine a middle school student escaping into the safety of his home after a hard day at school. He grabs a snack and goes up to his room—the safest place in his environment—and gets on his computer. There he receives an e-mail from an unfamiliar address, but he opens it anyway and finds a whole website devoted to him, or rather to humiliating him. There are cell phone photos of him changing in the boys' locker room and picking up books and papers after he had been shoved in the hallway, a bulletin board of humiliating comments from real and imaginary people, and a list of all the names he has been called. He doesn't know who did this, how they got his e-mail address, or even who to tell. His home is no longer safe, and the rest of the world is enemy territory.

Cyberbullying does not usually reach this level, though there are documented cases; however, it happens more often than we want to believe. These are the reported results from an i-SAFE survey done in the 2003–2004 school year with 1,500 students in grades 4–8 (children aged ten to fourteen years old):

- 42 percent of kids have been bullied while online. One in four have had it happen more than once.
- 35 percent of kids have been threatened online. Nearly one in five have had it happen more than once.
- 21 percent of kids have received mean or threatening e-mail or other messages.

- 58 percent have not told their parents or an adult about something mean or hurtful that happened to them online.[1]

By the time this book is published and in your hands, those statistics will be obsolete. "Cyber-bullying has increased in recent years. In a national survey of 10–17-year-olds, twice as many children indicated they had been victims and perpetrators of online harassment in 2005 compared with 2000."[2] Imagine what these statistics will show in 2010.

The Internet has changed most of what we thought we knew about bullying, and anonymity has leveled the playing field between the participants. The i-SAFE.org website provides the following information:

> The physical assault has been replaced by a 24 hour per day, seven days a week online bashing. Savvy students are using Instant Messaging, e-mails, chat rooms and websites they create to humiliate a peer. No longer can parents count on seeing the tell-tale physical signs of bullying—a black eye, bloody lip, torn clothes. But the damage done by cyber bullies is no less real, and can be infinitely more painful.[3]

The situation is complicated by the fact that most targets do not want to tell anyone because that will spread the word. Rarely do they go to an adult because they are ashamed to show the page to a parent or a teacher or a police officer.

Most adults are ignorant of the many cyberbullying varieties now being used. Nancy E. Willard in *Cyberbullying and Cyberthreats: Responding to the Challenge of Online Social Aggression, Threats and Distress* (Champaign, IL: Research Press, 2007), lists the following forms of cyberbullying:

- Flaming—Online confrontations with vulgar language
- Harassment—A continuous barrage of insulting, humiliating messages
- Denigration—"Dissing," posting gossip or rumors on other sites
- Impersonation—Pretending to be someone else, either a friend or the targeted person sending negative messages to others

- Outing—Sharing secrets or personal images online
- Trickery—Tricking someone into sharing personal infor- mation and then sharing it online
- Exclusion—Refusing participation in an online community
- Cyberstalking—Intense harassment, including threats[4]

The Canadian website www.cyberbullying.ca adds these to the growing list of ways to technologically harass or net-bully people:

- Chat rooms
- Small text messages—Cell phone and land lines
- Websites—The creation of a whole website targeting an individual inviting others to add comments
- Voting booths—A web page where other students can vote in different contests; for example, fattest, best butt, least likely to . . .
- Happy slapping—Physical assaults are recorded on cell phones and sent to other phones[5]

Though cyberbullying is the fastest growing form of bully- ing, traditional bullying happens more frequently and to more people. The books I have selected fit into two categories. Young adult books cover the full range of bullying, with cyberbullying being only one form of harassment. In *New Blood*, a cell phone captures bullies beating up the new kid, but when those photos are posted on a blog, the whole school sees them. In *Twisted*, Tyler, the targeted kid, gets blamed for everything, including the photos of Bethany posted all over the Web. *Shredderman* gives us Noland Byrd who takes on an Internet superhero persona to deal with the bully in his school.

Cyberbully books that deal with some form of electronic aggression include *The Truth about Truman School*, where two journalism students set up an online newspaper and decide not to censor anything. An anonymous person uses the site to attack and discredit one of the popular girls. In *Angels on Sunset Boule- vard* by Melissa de la Cruz, a website—TAP.com—becomes the hook that pulls teens into a cyber-cult. J. M. Steele's *The Market* refers to a website where each senior girl is a commodity whose stock is bought or sold, and Kate decides she wants to improve her ranking. In *Top 8*, Madison returns from a family vacation without any Internet connection to discover someone has stolen her identity and smeared all of her friends. They won't talk to her, and her boyfriend has started dating someone else. Her whole life has changed and she doesn't know who did it or why.

The Internet is a magical tool that seems to know everything and connects us to the whole world. It has changed our way of thinking, communicating, and learning, but we need to always remember the Internet is public space, not private space. If you wouldn't say it to a person's face, don't say it online.

FOCUS BOOKS

Picture Books

I could not find any picture books that deal with cyberbullying.

Intermediate

Shredderman by Wendelin Van Draanen, illustrated by Brian Biggs. New York: Alfred A. Knopf, 2004.

> Alvin:
> You're right—you do know me. I'm everyone you've ever beaten up or threatened. Everyone you've ever made fun of or robbed. You see me, all right. Every time you turn around. So look out. I'm watching.
> Yours in truth and justice,
> Shredderman (111)

Noland Byrd, a fifth grader, loves learning, but Bubba Bixby doesn't. Bubba likes to pick on other kids. He calls everyone names—Noland is Nerd, and there is a Bucktooth, Butthead, Moron, Toad, Fizz, and Worm Lips. Bubba also torments kids, steals things, and forces other kids to do his work. Once when Noland refused, Bubba hit him in the stomach.

Their teacher, Mr. Green, is really fun, but he doesn't believe Noland when he says Bubba is a bully. Every month, Mr. Green assigns a special project, and this month the special project is to create a newspaper page. The students can use their computers or paper and pens, take photos with a digital camera or draw illustrations. Each project would be different.

Noland decides to make a website instead of a newspaper page. He, Noland Byrd, will be the superhero Shredderman who will expose the injustice of Bubba Boy!

Kids who are bullied sometimes turn to the anonymity of cyberspace to get even with their tormentor, and there is a bit of that here. But with photos and a video Noland catches Bubba in the act of harassing the younger children in the cafeteria and lets his actions condemn him. The author carefully keeps Noland from becoming a cyberbully.

Topics for Discussion

1. How is Bubba an equal opportunity bully?
2. How do most of the students react to Bubba?
3. What are some things that show that Noland is really a very brave boy?
4. Who becomes Shredderman's sidekick?
5. When Bubba returns to school, he is even meaner. How do the students react to this meaner Bubba?
6. Do you think the teachers knew Bubba was a bully before they saw the evidence on the Shredderman website?
7. Not everyone can start a website to stop a bully. What is something you could do to help the targeted kids? To stop the bully?

Quotes for Reader Response

- Bubba Bixby was born big and mean, full of teeth and ready to bite. (1)
- Everyone's got two names: one from their parents and one from Bubba. (5–6)

- So I just eat lunch far away from him, make room when he's cutting in line, and let him call me Nerd. It's not fair, but at least I'm still alive. (6)
- How come a bully like Bubba had friends and I didn't? (33)
- And as I sat there catching my breath, I couldn't stop thinking about what I'd just done. How being Shredderman was making me do things that I'd only ever dreamed about before. (94)
- "So, tell me—what was so great about today?"
  "I . . . well, I stuck up for myself. Twice." (106)
- Calling him Bubba just feeds into that whole . . . *image* he's trying to build for himself. Don't enable him. Just call him Alvin. (116)
- "It's what you do when you think no one's looking that tells us what kind of person you really are." (118)
- But inside, I'm happy. Inside, I know I *can* find ways to fight for truth and justice. Inside, I know I *can* change the world—even if it's just my little corner of it. (138)

Middle School

The Truth about Truman School by Dori Hillestad Butler. Morton Grove, IL: Albert Whitman, 2008.

> *"Well, what could you expect from middle-school kids?" (66)*

Frustrated with their newspaper advisor and her refusal to print anything but "happy" articles, Zebby Bower and Amr Nasir start an underground newspaper on the Internet—www.truthabouttruman.com—where students will be able to read the truth about Truman Middle School. Zebby and Amr agree not to censor, even when an anonymous writer posting as milkandhoney starts a poll—"Who is the biggest poser at our school?" Clicking on that question brings up a fourth grade fat photo of Lilly Clarke, one of the ruling popular girls.

While Zebby and Amr are trying to write some legitimate articles and debating whether or not they should pull the Lilly Clarke stuff, other things are happening in the school. Trevor, a boy who has been bullied since early elementary school, is encouraged by the site and posts a cartoon strip. Sara Murphy has been called names and shunned since elementary school because of her eczema, so she has simply stopped talking. The plan seems to be working in her favor.

Lilly is not so lucky. The cyberbullying has progressed and now a page claiming to be from Lilly's private journal says she is ready to come out of the lesbian closet and tell all. Soon the other girls in her clique dump Lilly, and when the harassment spills over on them, they anonymously create another link to the "We Hate Lilly Clarke" page.

This book covers bullying on several different levels on and off the Internet. Lilly's secrecy about the harassment and refusal to tell her mom is typical behavior for a cyberbullied young person. And the fact that people will say more vicious things on the Internet, believing they could never get caught, fits the research about cyberbullying. One other thing that makes this book a major resource for this problem is that there is a real website at www.truthabouttruman.com where teens can go to get information about cyberbullying and share their stories. (The Internet contains many such resources.)

This book is a perfect fit for middle school.

Topics for Discussion

1. List all the bullying that goes on in this book. How does that list compare to your school?
2. Why do Zebby and Amr feel they have to allow the milk-andhoney postings?
3. Which bullying hurts Lilly the most, the cyberbullying or the abandonment by her friends?
4. Who is the cruelest person in the book? Explain your answer.
5. When Lilly dumps Zebby and Amr to join the popular girls, what does she do that hurt them the most?

6. How can bullying on the Internet be even more cruel than bullying in school?
7. What steps could Lilly have taken to be more proactive in dealing with this harassment?
8. What motivates milkandhoney to target Lilly?
9. It is unfortunately true that teachers, principals, and school staff generally do very little about the problem of bullying and even less about cyberbullying. How can this be explained?
10. How can teachers, principals, and school staff become more aware of bullying and cyberbullying?
11. What would you like your school to do to address these problems?

Quotes for Reader Response

- *Dear Lilly . . . I bet I can take one of the most popular girls at school and turn her into one of the most unpopular girls at school. And I bet I can do it without her, or anyone, figuring out who I am.* (44)
- The thing is, people like Lilly and Reece and the other popular kids could choose to use their powers for good. . . . They could just say, we're not going to pick on people anymore. And the whole school would follow their lead. But they don't do that. Instead they use their powers for evil. (54)
- With me, you don't joke about being a Muslim or being a terrorist; with Lilly you don't joke about her being fat. (63)
- But when you're in middle school, it matters a lot if you're gay. It matters a lot if people just think you're gay. It's like one of the worst things you can say about someone in middle school. (80)
- Who else would even dare take on someone in my group? (94)
- Teachers and counselors were usually the last to know anything. (117)
- "With the help of your Internet service provider, we were able to trace the IP address of this website to your home, Brianna." (142)

- "How come it's okay for adults to get new jobs and move away and even get divorced when they want out of something? But it's not okay when kids need a fresh start?" (160)
- The person you are when no one's looking, or when no one else knows who you are . . . that's the person you really are! (163)
- I got a little annoyed by how the teachers made such a big deal about this cyberbullying thing. Like cyberbullying was somehow worse than any other kind of bullying. Bullying is bullying. Whether it's being done on the computer or anywhere else. (163)

Angels on Sunset Boulevard by Melissa de la Cruz. New York: Simon and Schuster, 2007.

> *Taj shook her head, TAP—The Angels' Practice. It wasn't just a website. Or more specifically. The website was only the beginning. It was also a movement, a phenomenon, and a drug. Nobody knew what was in the drug, but its effects were astonishing—other worldly, like taking heroin, ecstasy, and acid all at once. (36)*

Taj and Johnny meet on TAP. com and find they share a love of music. After Johnny posts some songs on TAP, he becomes the overnight sensation of Johnny Silver. TAP has done it all, but TAP is more than just a social networking website. Like any Internet club, members can create their own profiles, enter chat rooms, and make connections. However, TAP has a gifting pyramid, where members can sign on to participate. New members buy gifts for those who have been members longer, to improve their status. Every other

Friday night, there is a TAP party at a different mansion in Los Angeles. Those in the highest circles are e-mailed a password that will get them into the private party, where you can drink an all-natural elixir that frees all inhibitions and participate in the secret ritual.

But there are too many mysteries. Johnny Silver disappears right before the audience's eyes, the members are getting younger, some teens are missing, and the ritual has attracted gawkers, but when someone wants out of TAP—that simply is not allowed. The masterminds, all teenagers, don't realize TAP has gone beyond community, free love, and fun to become a cult.

Topics for Discussion
1. List some of the positive things about TAP.com.
2. What makes TAP.com so tempting?
3. Taj says several times they asked for outrageous things just to see what would happen, like in Johnny's contract. What did happen?
4. How does Nick seem to keep from becoming too entangled?
5. Does TAP attract a particular crowd? Define what types of kids are most susceptible to TAP.
6. Who is Sutton Werner? He left town an outsider and came back a hero. What happened?
7. When Fish, Nick's sister, returns, she doesn't remember anything that happened to her during the time she was missing. Will she get involved with TAP again?
8. Is TAP.com an Internet cult? What do you see as its future?

Quotes for Reader Response
- To them, Johnny Silver was a hero. A rebel. An icon. A god. (19)
- Sutton had come into their lives just like any other fan, as a TAP request, . . . he had arranged the impromptu TAP parties, had been the one to bring the record label on board, had booked the Viper Room, had promised them . . . the world. (34)

- What was in or out was adopted and discarded so quickly, it was hard to keep up. Nick always wondered who decided what was cool to wear, to drink, to buy. And why did everyone follow so slavishly? (83)
- And the girl who'd gotten Tapped that night. She looked like she was about to faint when she saw the needle. The fear in her eyes! That had been painful to watch. And it wasn't supposed to be painful . . . it was supposed to be holy. A divine experience, shared with those who felt the same as you. (101–2)
- There were girls like Maxine who could never take rejection. Not even when they had caused it. They believed they deserved to be loved, to have everything in spite of their actions. Or that their actions had no consequences. (107)
- "Because she wanted to fit in, because she wanted to belong—that's why. . . . And she was so insecure she would pay to be accepted." (156)
- "The gossip—that was your brilliant idea, about controlling behavior. The wish lists. Creating a desire. Keeping the cows dumb. Keeping everyone content. Distracting them. So they don't see what's really out there." (217)
- "Fame is the new thing now. Did you know that sixty percent of America's teenagers believe they will become famous? For no reason at all." (220)
- "TAP is about loving everyone, not just one person. I'm sorry Nick," she said, as if she were reading from a script. Her eyes were blank and remote. (226)

ANNOTATED BIBLIOGRAPHY

Some books are appropriate for other levels; P = primary grades, I = intermediate grades, M = middle school, H = high school. Books discussed at length elsewhere in this text are noted parenthetically.

Picture Books

I could not find any picture books that deal with cyberbullying.

Intermediate

Abash and the Cyber-Bully by Matt Casper and Ted Dorsey. Los Angeles: Evergrow, 2008. This picture book/graphic novel is part of a series about Emotes—unique beings created out of the super-energy of all Internet users' emotions. Abash is the embarrassed Emote, and on the day he accidentally wears two left shoes to school, Imp, the mischievous Emote, takes his picture and posts it on the Net. (P)

The Revealers by Doug Wilhelm. New York: Farrar, Strauss and Giroux, 2003. Russell, Elliot, and Catalina have nowhere to go for help with the harassment each is enduring, until they band together and post the discrimination on the school's KidNet. (M)

Shredderman by Wendelin Van Draanen, illustrated by Brian Biggs. New York: Alfred A. Knopf, 2004. Fifth grader Noland Byrd decides to create an Internet Superhero, Shredderman, to deal with bullying and bully Bubba Bixby. (See page 152.)

Middle School

Chat Room by Kristin Butcher. Victoria, BC: Orca Currents, 2006. Ninth grader Linda tries to protect herself by being invisible, but then the school sets up a chat room on its closed website where she finds a place everyone can be anonymous and no one makes fun of her. Practicing in the chat room gives Linda the confidence to change her public behavior. (I)

Kiss & Blog by Alyson Noël. New York: St. Martin's Griffin, 2007. Winter and Sloan practice all summer to create perfect images for tenth grade, but when Sloan sees her chance to be the next Pink Princess, she not only ditches Winter, she turns the other sophomore girls against her. Winter starts an online blog where she journals her feelings, and though she never uses any names, everyone knows somebody who fits the Sloan role.

New Blood by Peter McPhee. Toronto: James Lorimer, 2007. After being viciously beaten by three older teens, fourteen-year-old Callum and his parents move from Scotland to Winnipeg where his older brother Ewan and his wife live. But on the first day of school, Callum's accent draws the attention of

Rick and his gang of thugs, and someone films Rick throwing Callum through the air and posts it on a blog site for the whole school to see. (H)

Queen of the Toilet Bowl by Frieda Wishinsky. Victoria, BC: Orca Soundings, 2005. Renata and her family left Brazil after her father died. Now in the United States of America, Renata works hard to be invisible in her elite school so nobody will discover her mother supports them by cleaning houses. But queen bee Liz finds out and floods the Internet with photos of Renata's mother with her head in a toilet bowl. The school deals with the situation immediately, and there is much verbal support for Renata's courage and horror about the "Internet bullying." (I)

The Secret Blog of Raisin Rodriguez by Judy Goldschmidt. New York: Penguin, 2005. Raisin and her little sister move from Los Angeles to Philadelphia after their mom remarries. As she tries to fit in with the most popular seventh grade girls, Raisin has one hilarious adventure after another. She writes them up in her blog, and of course, it accidentally gets spread throughout the entire school.

Something to Blog About by Shana Norris. New York: Amulet Books, 2008. Angel has bullied Libby since kindergarten and now in tenth grade it only gets worse when Libby's mom and Angel's dad start dating. At a peace dinner, Angel slips into Libby's bedroom and sends Libby's Internet journal out to everyone at school.

Sophie Loves Johnny by Nancy Rue. Grand Rapids: Zonderkidz, 2006. Seventh graders Sophie and Johnny attend a one-day workshop on the problem of cyberbullying. Back at school they create an informational school website to help people understand how to avoid cyberbullying and how to get help if it happens to them. The site is online just in time to help Sophie, who gets targeted through cell phones and the Internet. (I)

Top 8 by Katie Finn. New York: Scholastic, 2008. While Madison is on vacation with her family, someone hacks into her Friendverse account, takes on her identity, and spills all the gossip Maddie knows about her friends and enemies. It takes her a week of sleuthing to discover her best friend is the hacker. (H)

The Truth about Truman School by Dori Hillestad Bitler. Morton Grove, IL: Albert Whitman, 2008. Two students start an Internet newspaper where anyone can post the truth about their school, and they soon run into problems. Someone wants to destroy Lilly Clarke, the most popular girl in school, with anonymous postings. Lilly's friends abandon her, other anonymous sites attack her, and the school knows nothing about it. Everything from cyberbullying to personal responsibility to free press and more are covered in this book. (See page 154.)

High School

Angels on Sunset Boulevard by Melissa de la Cruz. New York: Simon and Schuster, 2007. TAP.com may have started out as a website but it has turned into an online cult with many rituals. Besides the closed parties in a password-guarded inner room, there is a pyramid structure that manipulates the newest member into expensive gift giving to established members in order to gain acceptance. Taj and Johnny were there at the beginning, but now Johnny has vanished and Taj realizes she's in too deep to get out. (See page 157.)

Burn by Suzanne Phillips. New York: Little, Brown, 2008. Cameron Grady suffers daily beating by the bullies, but one day the thugs go beyond their usual cruelty. Catching him in the locker room, they strip him, photograph his genitals, stroke him into an erection, and then photograph him again. By the time Cameron frees himself, the whole school has the cell phone images.

Good Girls by Laura Ruby. New York: Wendy Lamb Books, 2006. When Audrey realizes Luke DeSalvo is not good for her, she decides to end their relationship with "good-bye oral sex." She doesn't know that someone has opened the door and taken a photo until it shows up on everyone's cell phones and in her parents' e-mail.

The Market by J. M. Steele. New York: Hyperion Books, 2008. With third circle status in her high school, Kate Winthrop cannot understand why first circle Gretchen Tanner, Queen of the Proud Crowd, has called her "71." Within days she discovers a stock exchange–like website called the Market on which every girl in the senior class has been ranked. Kate's best friend Dev decides to help Kate improve her status. (M)

Raiders Night by Robert Lipsyte. New York: HarperCollins, 2006. Matt Rydeck, co-captain of the football team, too hazy from using steroids and other drugs, does little in reacting morally to the brutal hazing of a new guy that he witnesses on the last night of camp, Raiders Night. Ramp, the other co-captain and the attacker, uses the Internet to intimidate Matt and others on the team to keep their mouths shut. (See chapter 9, page 175.)

Secrets of My Suburban Life by Lauren Baratz-Logsted. New York: Simon Pulse, 2008. Having moved from New York City to Danbury, Connecticut, Ren E'Arc struggles to create a new life after her mother's sudden death. When she realizes Farrin, the most beautiful of the popular crowd, has connected with a cyber-stalker, Ren decides to save her by taking her identity in a sex website.

Twisted by Laurie Halse Anderson. New York: Viking, 2007. Tyler Miller used to be the invisible boy at school until he spray-painted the high school with obscenities and then became the high school weirdo. Not much of an improvement, except now most people left him alone, except Chip Milbury, elitist bully and brother to Tyler's heart's desire, Bethany. At a blowout party, photos are taken of Bethany, nearly naked and passed out, and posted all over the Internet. Tyler is blamed.

Professional Books

Cyberbullying and Cyberthreats: Responding to the Challenge of Online Social Aggression, Threats, and Distress by Nancy E. Willard. Champaign, IL: Research Press, 2007. The excellent resource provides everything a parent or a school system needs to know for cyber-safety and to start a comprehensive school program to deal with cyberbullying. This is my primary text resource.

Cyber-Safe Kids, Cyber-Savvy Teens: Helping Young People Learn to Use the Internet Safely and Responsibly by Nancy E. Willard. San Francisco: Jossey-Bass, 2007. Written to parents, this manual will answer all parents' questions as well as educate them on what they need to know and what they need to teach their children about the Internet.

Websites

Though I am a book lover, nothing challenges the Internet for up-to-date research, and these are my first choice sites for cyberbullying information. Having said that, I also know that by the time you read this page, these sites may have changed. There are more sites than I can review, so I have presented my favorites as of today.

www.cyberbullying.org (also www.cyberbullying.ca)

"Cyberbullying involves the use of information and communication technologies to support deliberate, repeated, and hostile behaviour by an individual or group, that is intended to harm others."—Bill Belsey, Canadian school teacher. This site grew out of Belsey's site, www.bullying.org, which went online in February of 2000 and is considered the number one website dealing with bullying.

www.isafe.org

"The goal is to educate students on how to avoid dangerous, inappropriate, or unlawful online behavior. i-SAFE accomplishes this through dynamic K–12 curriculum and community outreach programs to parents, law enforcement, and community leaders. It is the only Internet safety foundation to combine these elements." The last time I checked this website, it was very high tech and teen attractive, definitely a good training ground for adults.

www.bewebaware.ca

I have found Web Aware a very useful parent site, and I particularly like the safety tips for kids, starting with two- to four-year-olds and continuing up to fourteen to seventeen-year-olds. The FAQ page contains fifteen questions and answers that all parents need to know.

www.csriu.org

The Center for Safe and Responsible Internet Use was established to provide outreach services addressing issues of the safe and responsible use of the Internet. The creator, Nancy

E. Willard, maintains a blog on this site and has posted the notes from several of her presentations for our reference.
www.pewinternet.org (Pew Internet & American Life Project)
I found this site by accident when someone sent me their article, "Social Networking Websites and Teens." The mission statement defines the site as a "nonprofit 'fact tank' that provides information on the issues, attitudes and trends shaping America and the world. Pew Internet explores the impact of the Internet on children, families, communities, the work place, schools, health care and civic/political life. The Project is nonpartisan and takes no position on policy issues."
www.wiredkids.org
This colorful and interactive site's work involves preventing and helping investigate cybercrimes and abuses, but Wired Kids also has a softer side, with many online safety games for younger children. Helpful information for children of all ages, teachers, parents, and law enforcement can easily be accessed.
www.mindohfoundation.org
MindOH!, an e-learning company focused on character education, focuses on respect and responsibility in every facet of life. The site is another great place to educate yourself. I like the section on how to help kids stay safe on social networks.
www.netbullies.com
Though I found several weird spelling errors, this site has solid material and it offers direction to parents, kids, and schools, which need direction the most. I am hoping this site stays current, if only to help schools become more responsible.

NOTES

1. "Cyber Bullying: Statistics and Tips," i-SAFE, www.isafe.org/channels/sub.php?ch=op&sub_id=media_cyber_bullying (accessed November 4, 2008).
2. "11 Facts about Cyber-bullying," DoSomething.org, www.dosomething.org/tipsandtools/11-facts-about-cyber-bullying (accessed November 4, 2008).

3. "Cyber Bullying: Statistics and Tips," i-SAFE, www.isafe.org/channels/sub.php?ch=op&sub_id=media_cyber_bullying (accessed November 4, 2008)

4. Nancy Willard, *Cyberbullying and Cyberthreats: Responding to the Challenge of Online Social Aggression, Threats and Distress* (Champaign, IL: Research Press, 2007), Appendix K: Parent Guide to Cyberbullying and Cyberthreats, 265–67.

5. "Examples," Cyberbullying.ca, www.cyberbullying.ca (accessed November 4, 2008).

9

Violence:
Guns, Hazing, Bullycide

On October 9, 2008, when I googled "violence in school," there were 7,510,000 links. Six hours later there were 8,390,000. I surfed a small number of that 8 million plus, but too many of them wanted to protect students' right to bear arms. According to a report of the National Center for School Safety, in 2004 there were just ten student homicides at school. This makes the risk of homicide about 226 times greater outside of school than inside school.[1]

Violence in schools does not always mean shootings. In fact, guns are a very small part of the violence that happens in schools, but violence with guns makes headlines. There are far more students who are afraid of another student or a particular school environment (lunchroom, hallway, locker room, school bus) than there are students afraid of facing a gun in the school building. Those daily fears are not as attention getting—but they are far more real. The bullying events that make the news are the culmination of many smaller events; those smaller events are what we need to deal with. This is not an issue we can work backward on; we have to start early and work forward.

Initiation rituals are some of those events that need to be exposed early. Hazing grows out of those rituals and crosses the line out of membership qualifications and unity building into public humiliation and physical harm. The website www .StopHazing.org divides hazing into three levels—subtle, harassment, and violence. The subtle hazing "involves activities or attitudes that breach reasonable standards of mutual respect and places new members/rookies on the receiving end of ridicule, embarrassment, and/or humiliation tactics." Examples range from receiving demerits, obeying the orders of older members, and being tested on meaningless information. Harassment hazing involves "behaviors that cause emotional anguish or physical discomfort in order to feel like part of the group. Harassment hazing confuses, frustrates, and causes undue stress for new members/rookies." Examples of this type of hazing include verbal abuse, stunt nights, sleep deprivation, sexual simulations, and the expectation that one will harass others. Violent hazing can potentially "cause physical and/or emotional, or psychological harm." The examples all involve forced compliance with possible physical and/or legal consequences—paddling, branding, burning, public nudity, abductions, and alcohol or drug consumption.[2] Simply put, hazing is victimization. In Carrie Mac's *The Beckoners*, a girl gang initiates its members by branding them with a hot fork on the underside of their upper right arm. *Raiders Night* by Robert Lipsyte also contains violent hazing of a transfer student during football camp by a senior co-captain.

The word "bullycide" came into our language in 2001, defined as the suicide of a child that occurs after that child has been bullied or harassed. It's not just being bullied or harassed, but being bullied to the point where death is more welcome than another day of that bullying, that pain, that hopelessness. Seven mothers of teens who committed bullycide have created a website, www.bullycide.org, and written a book, *Bullycide in America*, containing their stories. *Thirteen Reasons Why* by Jay Asher, a haunting novel that tells Hannah's story of sexual harassment and bullying after she has committed suicide, is told in her voice through a series of audiotapes she left for those who destroyed her life. Covering three years, the book shows how the harassment started small and was actually directed at another girl but gave others permission to harass Hannah. Each action led to the next, more hateful action until her life was unbearable.

These are examples of the outer edge of bullying, and dealing with these behaviors are rescue attempts. Why should anyone be pushed to these extremes? What is wrong with our culture that we ignore all the steps that lead to such extreme bullying violence?

FOCUS BOOKS

Picture Books

Just One Flick of a Finger
by Marybeth Lorbiecki,
illustrated by David Diaz.
New York: Dial Books, 1996.

> *The rule*
> *at my school*
> *is you're a fool*
> *if you can't get*
> *your hand on a gun.*

Not many picture books deal with guns and violence, but this one not only covers the dangers and the consequences but also has incredible illustrations. Jack and his friend Sherms stick together against Reebo, a street-wise bully. Even though they make a blood pact, Jack wants a gun so he can feel more powerful. When Jack takes his dad's revolver to school, Sherms thinks he's crazy and leaves.

Topics for Discussion

1. Describe Jack and Sherms's school.
2. How does their school compare to yours?
3. Does Reebo bully both Jack and Sherms? Who does he focus on?
4. How will a gun help Jack?
5. How does Sherms react when he sees the revolver?
6. Reebo shows up, Jack flashes the gun, but who stops him?
7. Who is injured?
8. What is Lee's plan for Sherms and Jack?

Quotes for Reader Response

- Sherms, who has muscles where I have Twinkies edged between us. Still I got to thinking how I'd like a gun—

- "Coward!" Sherms muttered, "I thought you were somebody."
- "Fatty Boy loses his lunch," he hollered, . . . my brother, my only friend, had come to this end 'cause of me, me and that killing machine.
- "Straight as a church steeple and proud as a Masai."

Intermediate

I could not find any intermediate books about violence.

Middle School

Lockdown by Diane Tullson. Victoria, BC: Orca Soundings, 2008.

> *I watch Josh's face. When he stutters, it means he's stressed. When Josh gets stressed, he gets quiet. It reminds me of a storm, all the energy swirling in on itself. Once in a while Josh loses it, but it's amazing what he puts up with. The idiots of Science 10 have made this term a living hell for Josh. (11)*

In Adam's Science 10 class, the students wait for Ms. Topett's return under strict orders not to leave their seats, but the hamster has just had its babies. Soon they are all pushing around the cage. Josh, the quiet and often bullied kid, cares for the hamsters and doesn't want anyone near the cage to scare the mother and babies. Unfortunately, he doesn't have enough power to stop Chase, who pulls away the little shelter and shakes the cage. Ms. Topett arrives just as the mother hamster panics and kills the babies. Chase says, "So we scared it. Big deal." Josh silently glares at each of them and then walks out of the room. Adam, the only kid who has any kind of a relationship with Josh, watches him leave.

Later Adam and Zoe are in the hall almost flirting when the alarm bell goes off. Teachers come out of their classrooms shouting, "Lockdown, now!" They pull kids into their rooms and lock the doors. Adam and Zoe keep talking, amused that the teachers are making such a big deal out of another drill. Then Mr. Connor, the principal, comes over the PA and says that there is a gunman in the school. Suddenly the halls and stairs fill with hysterical students. Adam grabs Zoe and pulls her out of the rush. Doors are slamming, and as they run down the hallway, they hear gunshots. They run into a restroom and huddle on a toilet, when the shooter comes in. It's Josh.

After Josh shoots out the lights, he turns and leaves. Adam starts through the deserted hallways thinking he is the only one who could possibly talk to Josh.

This tension-filled, fast-reading story is played out too often in our newspaper headlines. Josh is not a hateful kid, just a kid who has been pushed too far by the cruelty of others.

Topics for Discussion

1. At the beginning of the book, what is Adam's opinion of Josh? Of Chase?
2. How do most students treat Josh? Why?
3. What kind of principal is Mr. Connor?
4. Everyone in the school has practiced what to do in a lockdown. When the lockdown is real, how does everyone behave?
5. After the bathroom scene, what motivates Adam to search out Josh?
6. Zoe wants Adam to stay hidden with her. When he doesn't, what does she do?
7. When Josh and Adam fight over the gun, whom is Josh trying to shoot?
8. Explain the term "suicide by cop."
9. Adam believes Josh never meant to kill anyone. What do you believe?

10. What has Josh prepared before he takes the gun to school? How does Josh involve Adam?

Quotes for Reader Response

- We're still laughing when we reach the bottom of the stairs. Two things happen at the exact same time. First, we see the stairwell doors chained and padlocked. Then we hear Mr. Connor's voice over the PA. He says, "This is not a drill. There is a gunman in the school." (32)
- I shout at him, "Not yet. Let us in!" He looks me straight in the eye and slams the door. I hear the lock thumping into place. (36)
- The shooter is Josh. The gun comes up. Maybe I'll stop the bullets. Maybe Baker won't get hit. Maybe Josh will shoot me and leave the others. I feel suddenly ice old. (44)
- "I didn't mean it was your fault. I mean, no one stepped in. So maybe it's everyone's fault. And anyway, Josh isn't crazy. He's just different."
  Baker nods. "Totally. Normal to the extreme." (41)
- When did it happen? When did he go from being just Josh to who he is now? (60)
- "Why now, Adam? Why step up now, when there's everything at stake?" (71)
- Everyone loves Zoe. Zoe can walk into a room full of strangers and just expect that people will like her. I don't think Josh has ever felt like that. (72)
- Two things happen at the same time. I hand the gun to Mr. Connor, and Josh lunges for it. More than two things, actually. Far more than two things, because as soon as Josh grabs for the gun, the officers open fire. (89)
- Almost normal. Normal to the extreme. (98)

Ricochet by Julie Gonzalez. New York: Delacorte Press, 2007.

And now here I am, wishing I could go to the library to get the answers I'm seeking. I wish life was that organized. Then I could type my subject into the card catalog, and the screen would flash up the many sources I could consult to fix my life . . . to make my world sane . . . to turn back the clock . . . to make it unhappen. (88)

Connor and Daniel have been friends since early elementary school. Now at fifteen they are still friends, but each also starts growing into new directions. One direction Daniel finds is Will Stanton. Connor believes Will is trouble, but that night he didn't know Will would join them or what Will had planned.

They go up the fire escape onto the roof of Will's building. He walks to an old chest of drawers, reaches underneath, and pulls out a silver revolver. "Russian roulette, anyone?"

One boy is killed and the others emotionally wounded in this incredible book that answers part of the question—why?

Topics for Discussion

1. Connor didn't want to play Russian Roulette; why did he?
2. It seems that what attracted Daniel to Will is the same thing that repelled Connor. What is it? What does it tell us about Daniel and Connor?
3. After Daniel is shot, Will smiles, walks over, and puts the gun in Daniel's pocket. Why does Will smile?
4. Why can't Connor stop thinking about that smile?
5. How do the members of Connor's family respond to him after the shooting?
6. The bullying in this book takes place early and leads to tragedy. What behaviors does the bully use to intimidate others?
7. Connor's mom thinks Jesse is a nice kid, but she is concerned about Steward. What has influenced her judgments?
8. Why does Connor revisit the roof?
9. Who is Quicksilver?

Quotes for Reader Response

- Will required victims. If you weren't his target, you didn't dare intervene or he'd aim his barbs at you. I'd been on the receiving end of his assaults often enough to know that his venom was bitter and cruel. (7)
- He fished a bullet from his shirt pocket and slipped it into one of the chambers. Then he twirled the cylinder. It hummed. "Russian roulette, anyone?" (21)
- "Sounds twisted to me," I said. "That's 'cause you're such a little wimp," Will sneered. "If you had any balls you'd do it." (23)
- "Do it." Will leaned toward Ryan with a sneer on his face. "What? You're too scared, little sissy girl." (29)
- Will victimized that kid regularly. He made loud sarcastic comments about the boy's clothes, shoes, or voice, and the poor kid blushed bright red. I felt ashamed to be sitting there, crippled by my silence. (36)
- Me. I'm fifteen and trapped in the middle. Neither gutsy nor golden, just quiet, dependable, unobtrusive. Of course, that was before. (40)
- I found an island in an ocean made of glass. The sole creature to visit me there was Quicksilver, the dragon king. (56)
- I lie in bed at night and it replays itself nonstop. I can't shut it off. And each time the same things happen. I keep thinking *if only this, if only that.* "It doesn't help to go there," he said. "To the land of if." (67)
- "I knew Will was bad news, but still . . . still . . . I let Daniel go with him. It eats at me in my sleepless hours. I should have kept him home that night." (114)
- The Quicksilver spoke one word to me, and although I did not understand his language, I understood what word it was. *Forgiveness.* (164)
- Then he sang my secret name and put Truth into my hands . . . Truth glowed brightly. It smelled of jasmine and blood and the ocean. But I was perplexed. Each time I held Truth, its colors and textures were different. But never was Truth black or white. (184)

High School

Raiders Night by Robert Lipsyte. New York: Harper-Collins, 2006.

If you can be a football player and a Raider, you'll know you're going to be one helluva man. (72)

Matt Rydell, Brody Heinz, Tyrell Williams, and Pete Torelli were the Back Pack. The four of them had played football together for a long time and nothing would stop them this year, their senior year. The Raiders would go all the way!

Matt had his sights set on the AFL. He and some of the others had been taking steroids for two years to build the body mass they believed they needed. So far the side effects weren't too bad, and the payoff was worth it. He and Ramp were co-captains. Matt didn't consider Ramp a friend, but he left that off the field. The story opens just before their final training camp: the week the guys would work together and come out a stronger, more powerful Raiders team.

From the beginning, Ramp didn't like the transfer kid, Chris Marin. Coming in as a sophomore, Chris would still be new, but he didn't act new, and Ramp didn't like that or that Chris was good enough to claim some of Ramp's glory. As co-captain, Matt stepped in and tried to keep things calm. But on Raiders Night, the last night of camp, after the coaches had left them to their Pride Night, Ramp takes things too far. Instead of just humiliating the new guys, Ramp rapes Chris with a plastic bat. Matt is paralyzed—but Tyrell charges forward, followed by Matt and Pete, who helps Chris to stand. As the seniors scream at each other, Chris escapes. The Back Pack hunts for him, but never finds him. No one knows what to do.

In the hours and days that follow, a conspiracy of silence settles over the team and the coaches. Chris is just a casualty on their way to a winning season, but their consciences catch up to them and the Back Pack finally does what is right.

Topics for Discussion

1. How does Matt define his responsibilities as co-captain? How does Ramp define his responsibilities as co-captain?
2. Ramp is after Chris from the moment he shows up. Why all the hate?
3. List all the chemicals Matt is putting into his body. How are they affecting him?
4. List all the bullies in the book. Do they share any characteristics?
5. How is Matt like his dad? What stops Matt from turning into his father?
6. Make a list of Ramp's harassing statements. What seems to be his main focus?
7. List everyone who is involved in the conspiracy of silence about Raiders Pride Night. Which name(s) surprises you?
8. How do Chris and the younger members of the team interpret that silence?
9. When bystanders or witnesses do nothing, how does the bully feel?
10. How does Ramp want his smear campaign to affect the Back Pack?

Quotes for Reader Response

- Matt nodded and felt the excitement rise. Perfect timing. Load up just before camp so the juice kicks in during the two-a-days when we really need it. (2)
- Watching them, Matt felt a surge of brotherhood. He felt even closer to them in here than in the weight room or on the field. Taking the shots proved their commitment to the team and to each other. We'll do whatever it takes to get bigger, get better, to win. (8)
- Ramp was a good captain for keeping the troops in line, but he couldn't leave his mean streak on the field. (21)

- Pete said, "Ramp's got a hard-on for the new kid already?"
  "We'll work it out on the field," said Matt. (42)
- They [coaches] must suspect something, thought Matt. But they didn't really want to know. Like steroids—don't ask, don't tell. There could be trouble over this. Hurt the team. (82)
- It was a good practice, maybe because they focused so hard to make Chris invisible. Nobody mentioned him. (94)
- "How you treat people is a very big deal." (97)
- He never bullied kids in school, like Ramp and his pals did. Once he even stopped a trash canning in the cafeteria, some football players having fun with a violin nerd. (130)
- The e-mail was from COACHRIGHT69. A picture came right up of Chris and Matt screwing. The heads didn't fit the bodies, which were doing it doggie style. Matt was on top. (152)
- "You know, a man does what it takes," said Ramp. "A captain makes sure every man can do what he needs to do when the shit hits."
  "A captain takes care of his men." (174)
- "I changed my mind," said Ramp. "We're not listening to this faggot. Hey Chrissy, what's your dad in jail for, little boys?" (185)
- "It's not going to go away."
  "It will if you keep your mouth shut." (225)
- A man does what it takes. (228)

Thirteen Reasons Why by Jay Asher. New York: Razorbill, 2007.

> *I hope you're ready, because I'm about to tell you the story of my life. More specifically, why my life ended. And if you're listening to these tapes, you're one of the reasons why. (7)*

New to the school, freshman Hannah Baker was hopeful, vulnerable, and anxious to connect and make friends. But that's the start of her story told from three years later in her junior year, after Hannah has committed suicide and left audiotapes to explain why.

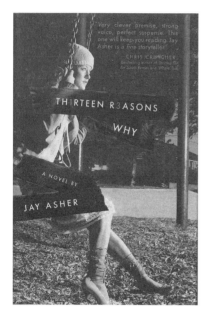

Asher lets Clay Jensen narrate the story as he listens to Hannah's voice on the tapes two weeks after she has died from an overdose. The tapes arrive in the mail, with no explanation, no return address, until she explains her directions as he listens. The story is really told through the eerie intertwining of their two voices, Hannah's through the earphones and into Clay's through his thoughts.

A kiss on the park playground with Justin, a boy she liked and who she believed liked her, turned into his opportunity to manufacture bragging rights with the guys. Then Alex, another supposed friend, adds Hannah's name to the *Freshman Class–Who's Hot/Who's Not* list. Hannah's name was beside Best Ass and established her as a target. The circumstantial evidence began to grow, which seemed to give boys liberties they had no right to. Grabs in the hall, cupped hands lingering on her bottom in stores, smirks from the hallway lineup of boys-pretending-to-be-men that happens in every school nurtured the rumors, and Hannah was permanently labeled. Only the teachers didn't know. Hannah tried to ignore the quiet voices and cruel words. It took three years before the growing assumptions isolated her, and wherever she reached out for help to NOT make the decision to die—she was let down.

Clay, an exceptional student, a respectful and responsible young man, might have been a nice friend for Hannah, but he was afraid of the rumors. While listening to Hannah explain the events that led her to suicide—his life and values change forever.

Asher has constructed the scaffolding of harassment based on the actions of thirteen specific people that led to the destruction of a human being. Sexual harassment is a form of bullying, and Hannah dies from a specific form of suicide—bullycide. Still too recent to be in most dictionaries, bullycide is being bullied to the point of suicide—when it hurts more to live with the constant bullying than it does to die.

Topics for Discussion

1. Hannah is given "Best Ass in the Freshman Class" status by one boy. What assumptions do others make based on that one non-fact?
2. What actions do others take based on that one non-fact? List them chronologically.
3. What part does male ego play in the book?
4. What might have happened if Clay had never believed the rumors? How might Hannah's life have been different?
5. Listening to the tapes, Clay realizes we each experience random connections every day. What are some examples of that in the book? From your life?
6. When Hannah refers to the snowball effect, what does she mean?
7. Give an example of the snowball effect from your life.
8. At what point does the damage to Hannah become irreversible?
9. Hannah repeatedly claims responsibility for her final act. Who else has some responsibility for her death?
10. How is Hannah a victim of bullycide?

Quotations for Reader Response

- *In the end, everything matters.* (13)
- *A rumor based on a kiss ruined a memory that I hoped would be special. A rumor based on a kiss started a reputation that other people believed in and reacted to. And sometimes, a rumor based on a kiss has a snowball effect.* (30–31)
- Only now do I realize that her reputation started in Justin Folley's imagination. (39)
- *Every single event documented here may never have happened had you, Alex, not written my name on that list. It's that simple.* (41)
- *I'm only playing, Hannah, Just relax.* (50)

- *Here's a tip. If you touch a girl, even as a joke, and she pushes you off, leave . . . her . . . alone. Don't touch her. Anywhere!* (52)
- After your visit, I twisted my blinds shut every night. I locked out the stars and I never saw lightning again. Each night, I simply turned out the lights and went to bed.
- *Why didn't you leave me alone . . . ?* (89)
- *And in high school, people are always watching so there's always a reason to pose.* (94)
- I'm listening to someone give up. Someone I knew. Someone I liked. I'm listening. But still, I'm too late. (146)
- *Bullies. Drugs. Self-image. Relationships. Everything was fair game in Peer Communications. Which, of course, made a lot of other teachers upset. It was a waste of time, they said. They wanted to teach us cold hard facts. They understood cold hard facts.* (155)
- How many secrets can there be at one school? (162)
- You can't go back to how things were. How you thought they were. All you really have . . . is now. (206)

SPECIAL RESOURCE BOOKS

Nonfiction

Bullycide in America: Moms Speak Out about the Bullying/Suicide Connection compiled by Brenda High. JBS Publishing Inc., 2007. E-book, www.bullycide.org

> *Bullying is a crime in which the perpetrators are rarely punished and the victims rarely receive justice.* (15)

Seven mothers tell their stories of their children's suicide; each one relates her child's harassment/torture, the escape of suicide, and then the slow recovery for herself and her family. In these stories, besides the common thread of bullying so powerful that it can push a young person to commit suicide, there are repeated examples of school systems that did not protect their students, particularly the targeted students, some through unforgivable ignorance and others due to stubborn arrogance. These are not acceptable excuses. Schools must create and enforce comprehensive anti-bullying programs that teach all students, K–12, and staff the importance of respect and that hold the adults in the school accountable for the safety of all students; this is not a problem for just the administrators to solve. These mothers do not just share their personal tragedy; they also have done their research and provide information on the following topics:

- Fighting the system
- Relational aggression
- Hazing
- Depression
- Cyberbullying

These women are the beginning of an army that will change school environments. They have already paid a very high price to get our attention. Only fools will not listen to them.

Letters to a Bullied Girl by Olivia Gardner with Emily and Sarah Buder. Foreword by Barbara Coloroso. New York: HarperCollins, 2008.

I was startled to find out that many anti-bullying programs have as their foundation nonviolent conflict resolution. But bullying is not about conflict, nor is it about anger. It is about contempt—a powerful feeling of dislike towards somebody considered worthless, inferior, or undeserving of respect. Contempt allows a bully

*to denigrate a peer and feel neither compassion for the target nor
shame for harm done. (xii)*

After the media released stories about how Olivia Gardner was
being bullied at her high school by nearly everyone, two sisters,
Emily and Sarah Buder, started a letter-writing campaign to support Olivia. The campaign spread from their school throughout
the state of California and gained media attention. This book
contains some of the over four thousand letters that people all
over the country sent to Olivia.

ANNOTATED BIBLIOGRAPHY

Some books are appropriate for other levels; I = intermediate
grades, M = middle school, H = high school. Books discussed at
length elsewhere in this text are noted parenthetically.

Picture Books

Hands Are Not for Hitting by Martine Agassi, illustrated by
    Marieka Heinlen. Minneapolis: Free Spirit, 2000. Children talk
    about all the things hands are for and what they are not for.
Just One Flick of a Finger by Marybeth Lorbiecki, illustrated
    by David Diaz. New York: Dial Books, 1996. Jack gets tired
    of being bullyied by Reebo and brings a gun to school, but
    instead of shooting Reebo, he accidentally shoots his best
    friend Sherms. (See page 169.)

Intermediate

I could not find any intermediate books about violence.

Middle School

Fighting: Deal with It without Coming to Blows by Elaine Slavens,
    illustrated by Steven Murray. Toronto: James Lorimer, 2004.
    Part of the Deal with It series, this workbook talks about
    how violence gets started, all the emotions that can get in the
    way, the Instigator, the Defender, the Witness, and Fighting
    101. All presented with colorful graphics. (H)

Lockdown by Diane Tullson. Victoria, BC: Orca Soundings, 2008. Thinking this lockdown is just another drill, Adam and Zoe do not worry when they are locked out of their classroom until the principal announces there is a gunman in the school. (See page 170.)

Pigboy by Vicki Grant. Victoria, BC: Orca Currents, 2006. Fourteen-year-old Dan Hogg is viciously bullied by Shane Coolen, and he just knows things will be worse when their class visits a pig farm. But who could have guessed an escaped convict would try to kill them all?

Project X by Jim Shepard. Alfred A. Knopf, 2004. Two inept, depressed, and angry eighth grade misfits decide to get back at their classmates and teachers by locking everyone into the gymnasium and shooting them. (H)

Ricochet by Julie Gonzalez. New York: Delacorte Press, 2007. Four boys are on a rooftop when one boy, Will, holds up a gun and suggests they play Russian roulette. They all make it through the first round, but then Will suggests they play idiot's roulette, and Daniel dies. (H) (See page 173.)

High School

The Battle of Jericho by Sharon Draper. New York: Atheneum, 2003. An invitation to join the Warriors of Distinction, the most exclusive club in school, carries prestige. However, Jericho has uncomfortable doubts when the initiation starts. At first everything seems honorable, but then the hazing gets dangerous. And Jericho's cousin dies.

The Beckoners by Carrie Mac. Victoria, BC: Orca Book Publishers, 2004. Zoe transfers to a new school where Beck and her violent gang seem to rule and torture April and other targets. Beck decides Zoe must join, but after she is branded with a burning fork, Zoe knows the Beckoners are not for her. (See chapter 5, page 86.)

Breaking Point by Alex Flinn. New York: HarperCollins, 2002. In a private school, rich students make life miserable for poor newcomers like Paul until Charlie, a school leader, invites Paul into his elite circle. Soon Paul realizes what that acceptance will cost him.

The Brothers Torres by Coert Voorhees. New York: Hyperion Books, 2008. Frankie has always looked up to his older brother Steve, but now Steve seems on a path contrary to all their family's values—he has joined the Cholos. As Frankie finds his path, he runs straight into his brother.

Bullycide in America: Moms Speak Out about the Bullying/ Suicide Connection compiled by Brenda High. JBS Publishing Inc., 2007. E-book, www.bullycide.org. Seven mothers whose children have committed bullycide tell their stories. (See page 180.)

Burn by Suzanne Phillips. New York: Little, Brown, 2008. Cameron Grady suffers a daily beating by the bullies, but one day the thugs go beyond their usual cruelty. Catching him in the locker room, they strip him, photograph his genitals, stroke him into an erection, photograph him again, and then send the images to everyone's cell phones. His rage and humiliation push Cameron into extreme violence.

Confidential Confessions: Volume 1, The Door by Reiko Momochi. Los Angeles: Tokyopop, 2003. At school, Manatsui lets others take advantage of her in order to fit in. She meets Asparagus, who cuts herself when the bullying gets too bad. Together they plan to commit suicide. Graphic novel.

The Dream Where Losers Go by Beth Goobie. Victoria, BC: Orca Book Publishers, 2006. Skey is in a lockdown unit after trying to commit suicide. When she is allowed to return to school, Jigger, her boyfriend and head of their gang, the Dragons, reenters her life. Slowly the memory of why she tried to kill herself resurfaces: she was gang raped at Jigger's instruction.

Endgame by Nancy Garden. Orlando: Harcourt, 2006. Fifteen-year-old Gray Wilton's past year of being bullied in school and intimidated by his father at home is revealed in his conversations with his lawyer as he awaits trial for bringing a gun to school and shooting several of his classmates. (M)

Eyes of the Emperor by Graham Salisbury. New York: Wendy Lamb Books, 2005. Just before the bombing of Pearl Harbor, a Hawaiian teenager of Japanese ancestry joins the U.S. Army, only to find himself and his Hawaiian comrades discriminated against, and then they are sent to a secret island in Mississippi where they become the bait for training attack dogs. (M)

Generation Dead by Daniel Waters. New York: Hyperion Books, 2008. Adam Layman, the biggest guy on the football team, and Phoebe Kindall, his best friend and goth-girl neighbor, approach their senior year with trepidation as the number of dead kids attending keeps growing. Now, Tommy Williams, a dead kid, has even tried out for football but the head coach has put out a hit on him! The prejudice in the school and community parallels all the real life prejudice that exists against minorities. (See chapter 3, page 43.)

The Ghost of Spirit Bear by Ben Mikaelsen. New York: Harper-Collins, 2008. When Cole and Peter return to their old high school in Minneapolis after their wilderness ordeals, they are faced with vicious bullying and a school administration that seems powerless, until they decide to be responsible for their own future. (M)

In the Garage by Alma Fullerton. Calgary: Red Deer Press, 2006. BJ and Alex had been best friends for eight years, but Alex couldn't share his most private secret with her. Told in flash-backs from Alex's funeral after he was beaten to death by a student mob. (M) (See chapter 7, page 138.)

Letters to a Bullied Girl by Olivia Gardner with Emily and Sarah Buder. New York: HarperCollins, 2008. After the bullying of Olivia Gardner made the news, two sisters started a letter writing campaign to show her she was not alone. (M) (See page 181.)

Names Will Never Hurt Me by Jaime Adoff. New York: Dutton Children's Books, 2004. A view of what happens in a high school on the one-year anniversary of a school shooting. The story is told in prose and verse, mostly from the perspectives of four teenagers, all of whom have been victims of harass-ment in various forms.

Raiders Night by Robert Lipsyte. New York: HarperCollins, 2006. Matt Rydell, co-captain of the football team, tries to forget what he witnessed on the last night of football camp when the hazing went too far and a player was raped. (See page 175.)

Shattering Glass by Gail Giles. Brookfield, CT: Roaring Book Press, 2002. Rob is the charismatic kid who moves to town and becomes the new leader for the males. He manipulates losers into the top clique and former winners into loser sta-tus. From the opening page, the reader knows who will die and wonders why the boys all go along with Rob's plan. (See chapter 5, page 88.)

Things Change by Patrick Jones. New York: Walker, 2004. Responsible and obedient Johanna, one of the top students in her high school class, gets involved with Paul, a fun-loving irresponsible senior who seems to adore her. But Paul slowly becomes possessive and then violent, and Johanna has a hard time breaking away.

Thirteen Reasons Why by Jay Asher. New York: Razorbill, 2007. Hannah Baker has committed suicide because it hurt too much to live. She has left behind a set of thirteen audiotapes to be delivered to and listened to by each of the people who contributed to her death. (See page 177.)

The Throwaway Piece by Jo Ann Yolanda Hernandez. Houston: Arte Publico Press, 2006. After years of taking care of her alcoholic mother, Jewel, a gifted loner, becomes a "state kid" when her mother abandons her for a string of loser boyfriends. Jewel finds herself on a self-destructive path for survival.

NOTES

1. National Center for School Safety, "Serious Violent Crimes in Schools," Youth Violence Project, youthviolence.edschool.virginia.edu/violence-in-schools/school-shootings.html (accessed October 9, 2008).
2. "Hazing Defined," StopHazing.org, www.stophazing.org/definition.html (accessed October 9, 2008).

Index

Wings, 22, 48
Winterman, Denise, 125, 126,
    148n2
Wishinsky, Frieda, 53, 96, 161
Wittlinger, Ellen, 24, 147
Wolfson, Jill, 28, 36, 49
Wong, Janet S., 50
Woodson, Jacqueline, 49, 103, 117

Yang, Gene, 119
Yankee Girl, 118

Yellow Line, 101, 108–10, 121
Yes We Can, 48
Yoon and the Jade Bracelet,
    33–34, 48, 91
Young, Diane, 99

Zarr, Sara, 25, 58, 78
"Zero Indifference: A How-to
    Guide to Ending Name-Calling
    in Schools," 148n1
Zindel, Lizabeth, 99

About the Author

C. J. Bott taught high school English for thirty years and still loved her job when she retired—but it was time to do something more about bullying. In 2004, her book *The Bully in the Book and in the Classroom* (Scarecrow Press) introduced the idea of using books with the theme of bullying to work with students from preschool to high school. It is her hope that this second book will not only provide more titles of bully books but also educate teachers and librarians with a broader awareness of specific types or targets of bullying, as each chapter focuses on a different bullying behavior. Through her books, her presentations, and her articles, C. J. wants to start the dialogue about bullying in hopes of arming our children with a greater awareness and more prevention skills.

C. J. lives in Solon, Ohio, with her husband, Don Gallo, and can be reached through her website, www.bulliesinbooks.com.